C.S. LEWIS AND THE FEELING INTELLECT

BRIGHT SHADOW OF REALITY

by Corbin Scott Carnell

William B. Eerdmans
Publishing Company   Grand Rapids, Michigan

Copyright ©1974 by William B. Eerdmans Pub. Co.
All Rights Reserved
Printed in the U.S.A.

Library of Congress Cataloging in Publication Data

Carnell, Corbin S
  Bright shadow of reality.

  Bibliography: p. 165
  1. Lewis, Clive Staples, 1898-1963—Criticism and
interpretation.   I. Title.
PR6023.E926Z6   828'.9'1209   74-725
ISBN 0-8028-1561-8

For Carol—without whom I'd be a sad, wayfaring pilgrim
— and for those students and colleagues from whom I've
learned about Lewis. I want to name the following in
addition to those authors listed in the bibliography:

John Abbott
Jim Anthony
Sigrid Bango
Ann Bates
Faith Bedford
Ed Berckman
Ray Binder
Bob Bryan
Linda Bryant
Charles Caldwell
Jim Campbell
Rick Carnell
Alburey Castell
Fred Castor
Dave Chilcoat
Catherine Chisholm
Andrea Coe
Bill Cole
Mardi Coleman
Fred Conner
Dick Cornelsen
Daniel Corrigan
Jerry Cullum
Jack Day
Maria Del Rio
David Dobson
Chip Dodson
Mara Donaldson
"Lawrence Dorr"
Ron Doyle
Hank Dunn
Lucy Erstling
Martha Fabrick
Ken Ferguson
Mike Fleishman

David Foerster
Winifred Frazer
Norma Neal Gause
Robin Gold
Clay Goodhnight
Bob Goodstein
Sally Green
Sam Hankin
Sheila Harrigan
Dick Hiers
Rob Hirshfield
Ron Hooks
Bill Hunt
Harriet Kavanagh
Ron Keller
Luis Andres Kidder
Hope Kirkpatrick
Steve Kraftchick
Ellie Kuypers
Jeff Jones
St. Julian Lachicotte
Karen Leader
Sherry Lefkowitz
Susan Lewis
Bill Lillycrop
Michael Mahoney
Steve Marko
Mary May
Dee McAfee
Bob McAllister
Charles McCoy
Eugene McGovern
Helen Louise McGuffie
Patricia McKenzie
Roy Mercer

Dave Milhouser
Marjie Miller
Albert Mollegen
Lois Newman
Henry Noel
Ants Oras
Earle Page
Frank Pajares
Lynn Pappas
Dan Parker
Ralph and Nancy Penland
Connie Penley
Ben Pickard
Jon Pott
Grace Preedy
John Price
Bernard Ramm
Bob and Martha Rankin
Jim Rayburn
Scott Rivers
Joe Rochelle
Beth Roffelsen
Martha Rutland
Forrest Sawyer
Arcadia Schaeper
Les Scott
Taylor Scott
Sue Scranton
Jim Seale
David G. Smith
Kathleen Smith
Sherlee Souders
Rheua Stakely
Dave Stanford
David Stryker

Joanne Swanson	Herb Wagemaker	Toby Williams
Camille Symons	Fran Ward	Ed Wilson
John Talbird	Bob Westbrook	Ted Wolf
Suzanne Thiems	Rosemary Widman	Mervin and Rosemary Ziegler
Sarah Thomson	Elisabeth Wilkinson	Stephanie Zisk
Paul Van Buren	Brent Williams	Bernie Zuber

Acknowledgments

The courtesy of the following publishers and individuals in permitting the use of several lengthy passages is gratefully acknowledged:

Harcourt Brace Jovanovich, Inc.: "The Apologist's Evening Prayer," from *Poems* by C. S. Lewis edited by Walter Hooper, copyright © 1964 by the Executors of the Estate of C. S. Lewis;

Harcourt Brace Jovanovich, Inc.: C. S. Lewis, *Surprised by Joy: The Shape of My Early Life*, 1956;

Harper and Brothers: C. S. Lewis' preface to *The Hierarchy of Heaven and Earth: A New Diagram of Man in the Universe* by D. E. Harding, 1952;

The Macmillan Company: C. S. Lewis, *George Macdonald: An Anthology*, 1947; *That Hideous Strength: A Fairy-Tale for Grown-Ups*, 1946;

Oxford University Press: C. S. Lewis, *Rehabilitations and Other Essays*, 1939;

Charles Scribner's Sons: Thomas Wolfe, *Look Homeward Angel*, copyright 1929 Charles Scribner's Sons; renewal copyright © 1957 Edward C. Aswell, as administrator, C. T. A. of the estate of Thomas Wolfe, and/or Fred W. Wolfe.

Effort, and expectation, and desire
And something evermore about to be.
                    —Wordsworth, *The Prelude,* VI

When we are lost in the woods
the sight of a signpost is a great matter.
                    —C. S. Lewis, *Surprised by Joy*

Contents

Preface

I have been fortunate in this research to be working with those who are interested in philosophy and theology as well as literature. Because so much of recent literary study inevitably moves onto a theological level, the territory shared by art and theology is no longer a no-man's land where specialists fear to tread. The scholar works empirically, yes, but what Tillich calls "ultimate concern" eventually shapes one's attitude toward his material. And he must, consciously or not, subscribe to some sort of ontology.

The necessity of seeing literature within the frame of an ontological system becomes obvious when one turns to the kind of literature examined in this study. Much of it reflects the approach which challenged Coleridge in the *Lyrical Ballads*—he wanted to make the supernatural seem real. Most modern writers who can be considered religious (in Tillich's sense of having strong convictions about ultimate values) prefer Wordsworth's approach, that of trying to make the real seem supernatural. Graham Greene, Joyce, Faulkner, Wolfe, and others have given us Realism, with profound implications about values. But only a few writers have attempted to describe the supernatural—it is too dangerous an undertaking.

I was first attracted to "supernatural" literature while engaged in a study of George Macdonald, under the direction of Professor Jerome Buckley at Columbia. Later I became interested in C. S. Lewis' fiction, especially as it

11

reflected his interpretation of the Romantic quest, and went to Florida to work with Professor Nathan Starr. His knowledge of Lewis' work gave me the impetus I needed to begin exploring the nebulous-looking concept my curiosity would not let me ignore, and that concept, C. S. Lewis' theory of *Sehnsucht,* or "the dialectic of desire," as he has called it, became the subject of this study.

I would like to express my appreciation to Chad Walsh for his initial encouragement; in fact, without his *C. S. Lewis: Apostle to the Skeptics,* I would not have begun this study. I would also like to thank Professor Clyde Kilby of Wheaton College for exciting and encouraging my interest in Lewis. And I especially want to thank Mrs. Joel McClatchey, curator of the large Lewis Collection at Wheaton, for her assistance.

Finally, I would like to warn the reader not to identify the subject of this study with the common interpretation of the word *Sehnsucht,* i. e., "nostalgia." With this usual translation in mind, Matthew Arnold called *Sehnsucht* a "wistful, soft, tearful longing."[1] It has a broader meaning in my title, this meaning being derived from Lewis' special use of the word. Thus it encompasses not only the Germanic longing Arnold describes but also the more turbulent, passionate aspiration associated with what Arnold calls "Celtic Titanism." In Chapter I, I have taken pains to describe the attitude which is the subject of my study, so if the reader is baffled by the term, he should take his courage in his hands and face with me that which so stubbornly resists being put into words. At times one sees it clearly, at other times it seems to recede before one's eyes. Like the palace of Cupid in *Till We Have Faces,* it is alternately visible and invisible. Thus, the exploring of this mystery has turned out to be a quest in itself.

Corbin Scott Carnell
English Faculty
University of Florida

[1] *On the Study of Celtic Literature* (New York: Macmillan, 1907), pp. 117-118.

I ›*SEHNSUCHT*

He groped for the doorless land of faery, that illimitable haunted
country that opened somewhere below a leaf or a stone.

—Thomas Wolfe, *Look Homeward Angel*

This is a study of an attitude which has been responsible
for some of the most powerful, and some of the most
controversial, works of literature. It may be tentatively set
forth as a special kind of longing—a longing difficult to
describe, for two reasons: it is surrounded by a misty
indefiniteness which seems essential to its very nature, and
second, there are overtones of sentiment and emotion in
certain expressions of the attitude which may seem mawk-
ish when examined in cold prose.

Yet the fact that this state of mind is difficult to
examine does not necessarily subtract anything from its
validity as a recurrent theme in literature. For many writers
it is simply there and they make no attempt to explain it.
Some of them—especially poets like Wordsworth and
Traherne—have expressed this attitude primarily as an ecstatic desire for union with nature; some have spoken of a
"sweet melancholy" which seems to have no cause; and
others have told of a relentless urge that leads men on in
pursuit of shadows. The terms of description seem quite
dissimilar at first. But once we grant that these may be
descriptions of the same thing, seen from different points

of view or in different moods, there opens before us a broad vista which invites exploration. Several years ago I began to wonder if these indefinite longings might reveal some underlying pattern, might indeed point to some basic similarity and continuity in human experience. Since then my thinking on the subject has crystallized in reading the works of C. S. Lewis.

Lewis was without doubt one of the most adventurous and learned men of the twentieth century. His interests and accomplishments ranged over wide areas—poetry, criticism, fiction, theology—and he dared to assert the marvelous and devout in an age which often rejected them. One can begin to read him as an undergraduate and go on reading him without ever feeling that he has left a favorite author behind, that he has outgrown him. He first attracted my attention in connection with this study because he was, to my knowledge, the first literary critic to give a name to the basic attitude which is my subject. I discovered further that in his critical writing he attempted a clear definition which differentiates this attitude from the various forms of "Romanticism." And in his fiction and poetry he set forth excellent imaginative expressions of the attitude. That is why most of this study will be devoted to the works of C. S. Lewis—in theory and in practice he has illuminated the theory better than anyone I know.

In several places Lewis has referred to the state of mind under discussion as *Sehnsucht.* I follow him in this choice of term because the German word has overtones of nostalgia and longing not to be found in any English word. Also, unlike such terms as "mystical" and "romantic," it has the advantage of not being overburdened by connotations. Most of my study will be concerned with Lewis' treatment of this theme in his own writings, but in order to explain the relevance of the attitude for literature in general, I would like first to give some of my own observations.

Sehnsucht, which literally means "longing" or "yearning," is both romantic and mystical in our present use of those words. It is, however, a good deal more specific than such terms. As I shall attempt to show presently, it may indeed represent an aspect of Romanticism, but it remains a basic attitude which may be part of other things without being equated with them. As an attitude it involves both an emotional reaction and an assessment of that emotional reaction, that is, a state of mind. Just what the emotions are and how they are produced are problematical matters which can be left for psychologists to investigate.[1] The state of mind, however, is something which can be analyzed intelligibly, and I believe profitably, by the student of literature.

The crucial concept in defining this attitude is best expressed in English by the word "nostalgia." Even though *Sehnsucht* may be made up of several components or appear in different forms (melancholy, wonder, yearning, etc.), basic to its various manifestations is an underlying sense of displacement or alienation from what is desired. In order to show how this sense of displacement forms the basis for the attitude, I would like to attempt a definition by the old technique of taking the thing apart.

Sehnsucht *and the numinous*

Many writers have seen in nature some evidence for the existence of a divine being, and this awareness has come not only in her sunnier, more benevolent aspects. As Rudolf Otto has pointed out in *The Idea of the Holy,* the awareness of the holy or the divine (which he calls the "numinous") comes often in fear, in awed surmise, in the hush of the deep mystery of man's finitude and creatureliness.

This notion recurs in literature. It goes back to "The Seafarer" and "The Wanderer" in English literature and can be found in the ancients as well. In the Old Testament, Jahweh is "a consuming fire," a being awful in his jealousy, majestic in his mystery. The human reaction to such a being is summed up in Isaiah's words: "Woe is me! for I am undone; because I am a man of unclean lips and I dwell in the midst of a people of unclean lips." The writer of the Book of Job also speaks of the incomprehensible

---

[1] I will, however, be inquiring into the psychological explanations, particularly in Chapter VI.

otherness of the Almighty, while Homer and the Greek tragic playwrights see a mysterious power overruling the wishes of the Olympian deities for reasons beyond human ken.

Here we have the reverse of the so-called Wordsworthian concept of God-in-Nature, not a divinity who beneficently sustains and restores man in nature, but a *mysterium tremendum* whose workings are unknowable and inexorable. Man in the face of such power is an overwhelmingly small and fragile thing.

Anthropologists have found that the deities of primitive cultures are thought of almost invariably as fierce and capricious; man is continually under threat of punishment or alienation from the gods. It is interesting that even since the rise of modern science, which has brought a large measure of control and understanding of the forces of nature, this feeling persists. William Blake, who lived two centuries after Galileo, Kepler, and Descartes, had a vivid awareness of the numinous. This is expressed throughout his work but with peculiar clarity in "The Tiger":

> Tiger! Tiger! burning bright
> In the forests of the night,
> What immortal hand or eye
> Could frame thy fearful symmetry?

The tiger is not an embodiment of evil but something Blake finds both admirable and fearful.

Wordsworth was also puzzled and disturbed by nature's dark, incomprehensible aspects. In the stolen-boat passage of *The Prelude,* he tells how a huge peak "upreared its head" and seemed to pursue him, growing in stature until it towered between him and the stars, how he was oppressed for days afterward "with a dim and undetermined sense / of unknown modes of being" (I, 357-400). And in "Tintern Abbey" he speaks of his boyhood as haunted by "the sounding cataract . . . the tall rock, the mountain, and the deep and gloomy wood." He senses in nature a divine presence which sustains all things, filling him with "intimations of immortality," but there are also hidden depths in nature which have an awesome and even terrible aspect. In the tenth book of *The Prelude* he tells of the impression made upon him by the French Revolution, how the very tremendousness of the time became a revelation of the holy and the divine:

> So, with devout humility be it said,
> So, did a portion of that spirit fall
> On me uplifted from the vantage ground
> Of pity and sorrow to a state of being
> That through the time's exceeding fierceness saw
> Glimpses of retribution, terrible,
> And in the order of sublime behests:
> But, even if that were not, amid the awe
> Of unintelligible chastisement,
> Not only acquiescences of faith
> Survived, but daring sympathies with power,
> Motions not treacherous or profane, else why
> Within the folds of no ungentle breast
> Their dread vibration to this hour prolonged?
> (X, 436-462)

Even to Wordsworth, whose view of the world is sanguine and optimistic beside that of Tennyson, Hardy, and others who were to become preoccupied with nature's fiercer aspects, man is to no small extent alienated from the good and the holy. His "Immortality" ode seems to suggest that it is the purity and innocence of childhood that is lost.

> There was a time when meadow, grove, and stream
> The earth, and every common sight,
> To me did seem
> Apparelled in celestial light,
> The glory and the freshness of a dream.
> It is not now as it has been of yore;—
> . . . .
> . . . there hath passed away a glory from the earth.

No theological reading of Wordsworth can escape his ambivalence on this point. Humanity senses the divine but is separated from it also. In Wordsworth's thinking, this separation is due less to the otherness of the deity than to certain defects in man and society, but the concept of displacement or nostalgia for another and better life is nevertheless present here.

Sehnsucht *and romantic longing*

The sense of exile is a note often sounded in the works of Romantic authors. Frank Kermode in *The Romantic Image* says that one of the two indispensable elements of Romanticism is a sense of isolation. (The other is characteristic use of the image.) This feeling of isolation is prominent in Byron, Shelley, Tennyson, and Arnold—right down to such recent figures as Thomas Wolfe. Though quite different from the nineteenth-century Romantics, Wolfe has given us the record of an agonizing struggle with the numinous and with a lonely, aching sense of disorientation. In *Look Homeward Angel* the rhapsodic lists of foods, places, and the glories of America are followed again and again by the words, "O lost." The world is strangely beautiful, life is filled with innumerable wonders, yet

> Naked and alone we came into exile. In her dark womb we did not know our mother's face, from the prison of her flesh have we come into the unspeakable and incommunicable prison of this earth. Which of us has known his brother? Which of us has looked into his father's heart? Which of us has not remained forever prison-pent? Which of us is not forever a stranger and alone. . . . Lost! Remembering speechlessly we seek the great forgotten language, the lost lane-end into heaven . . . an unfound door.[2]

At the death-bed of his brother Ben, Eugene Gant, who did not believe in God nor in Heaven or Hell, nevertheless felt that he must pray.

> He did not believe in angels with soft faces and bright wings, but he believed in the dark spirits that hovered above the heads of lonely men. . . . All that he had read in books, all the tranquil wisdom he had professed so glibly in his philosophy courses . . . left him now, under the mastering urge of his wild Celtic superstition. . . . So, with insane sing-song repetition, he began

---

[2] *Look Homeward Angel* (New York: Scribner's, 1929), frontispiece.

to mutter over and over again: "Whoever You Are, be good to Ben tonight. Show him the way."[3]

Eugene invokes the mercy of the "Other and Outer" even when intellectually he has rejected the idea of its existence. The numinous is awful, even threatening, and yet now it is, paradoxically, his last solace. Has it always been thus? Perhaps the gods had once been close to men, as in the stories of the Silver Age. Or was it to be in an age to come?

The Anglo-Saxon poet who wrote "The Wanderer" remembers happier times in his lord's bright mead-hall, Wordsworth remembers his childhood and youth, Gatsby stares at the green light on Daisy's dock, and Wolfe dreams of what America may be. The overwhelming sense of exile and loss can be borne only in nostalgic memories of the past or in visions of the future.

Ecstatic wonder

Surprisingly, man's awareness of the numinous has a close relation to that sense of happier wonder of which the poets write when they tell us of love, of the coming of spring, or the birth of a child. But while the sense of the numinous may involve fear and confusion at man's baseness or finitude in the presence of the divine, the wonder of spring, on the other hand, may bring feelings of ecstasy which cause the individual for the moment to transcend himself. (I am thinking of ecstasy in its etymological meaning: to stand outside oneself.) Such moments are rare; they may come with a mounting sense of grandeur in the presence of natural beauty or with piercing sweetness on hearing a certain strain of music. It may be a dance, a painting, or a chorale which awakens this feeling of aesthetic exaltation. In any case, the sense of displacement may again be observed—not a sense of alienation from a powerful and holy presence (the numinous) but an experience of "enormous bliss," of being transported to awesome heights which make the close-by world seem far

3 *Ibid.*, p. 556.

away. The individual feels that he is becoming one with the universe and desires an even closer union.

We find this note frequently sounded by poets of the Romantic Revival—especially Wordsworth, Shelley, and Keats—and by the American Transcendentalists—notably Emerson and Whitman. The following lines from Whitman's "Passage to India" voice this mood:

> O we can wait no longer,
> We too take ship O soul
> Joyous we too launch out on trackless seas,
> Fearless for unknown shores on waves of ecstasy to sail,
> . . . .
> With a laugh and many a kiss,
> (Let others deprecate, let others weep for sin, remorse, humiliation,)
> . . . .
> Bathe me O God in thee, mounting to thee
> I and my soul to range in range of thee.

The experience is one of exhilaration and questing. It could be called *Sehnsucht* in its happiest form.

Causeless melancholy

In *Journey to Java* Sir Harold Nicolson investigates a subject which shows us yet another side of *Sehnsucht*. He calls this emotion "causeless melancholy" and studies its expression in the works of "typical malcontents" from Galen and Lucretius to Rousseau, Kierkegaard, and Baudelaire. Though I am skeptical about some of Nicolson's conclusions (see Chapter VI of this study), I believe he deals with a highly important phenomenon in literature—one which has sometimes led to a stylized attitude, as in the "white melancholy" of "Il Penseroso," but which often is expressed with deep concern and personal involvement. We find it on many levels: the adolescent *Weltschmerz* of young Werther, the poetry of sentiment with its idle tears whose meaning is unknown, or the awareness of isolation which may suddenly strike the individual in common daily events, as in Arnold's poem, "The Buried Life":

But often, in the world's most crowded streets,
But often, in the din of strife,
There rises an unspeakable desire
After the knowledge of our buried life;
A thirst to spend our fire and restless force
In tracking out our true, original course;
. . . .
And many a man in his own breast delves,
But deep enough, alas! none ever mines.
. . . .
Yet still, from time to time, vague and forlorn,
From soul's subterranean depth upborne
As from an infinitely distant land,
Come airs, and floating echoes, and convey
A melancholy into all our day.

Not infrequently the locus of melancholy is fixed upon someone who is loved but does not return love, or on some ideal person who has died, or upon some golden time which is no more—the glory of Greece, the grandeur of Renaissance Italy, the mystic charm of the Middle Ages.

Yet with this much explanation, one might still say that this melancholy is "causeless," for its locus may be partly or completely fictitious, since it serves as a kind of outlet for the inevitable conflict between desire and nonfulfillment. In other words, causeless melancholy may be viewed as a way of achieving a tragic sense which will find expression even among "well-adjusted" people who live under reasonably happy circumstances.[4]

Novalis once said that philosophy is man's attempt to be at home everywhere. If that is so, perhaps causeless melancholy is the result of his inability to be at home anywhere.

The Blue Flower motif

A final aspect of *Sehnsucht* to be considered here is closely related to melancholic longing. But in this case, the pursuit of the unattainable—since the object of pursuit keeps ap-

[4] See Nicolson's discussion on this point in his *Journey to Java* (London: Constable, 1957), pp. 234-235. He finds that there are those given to melancholy who enjoy good health and freedom from serious trouble (e. g.,

pearing under the guise of the attainable—does provide a limited source of pleasure. The dreamer keeps on creating better worlds—in other places, among different people, etc. This motif is found in German literature as the search for the *Blaue Blume* and in Scandinavian ballads dating back to the Middle Ages as the *Längtans Bläa Blomma* (the Blue Flower of Longing).

Even since the rise of Naturalism in literature, the motif continues to appear—in such unexpected places as Dreiser's *Sister Carrie*, whose cosmos makes of metaphysics only a "psycho-chemical" product. The novel ends on a mysterious note which serves well to illustrate this old expression of *Sehnsucht.* Carrie, having reached a surprising degree of success, sits alone in her room, rocking. The two-bit jobs, the liaison with Drouet, the sordid marriage to Hurstwood are all behind her; she is now a theatrical star, well-to-do, sought after—but she still waits "for that halcyon day" when she will "be led forth among dreams become real." Then Dreiser concludes with a passage which, though verging on a mock-heroic kind of sentimentality, is remarkably penetrating:

> Oh, Carrie, Carrie; Oh blind strivings of the human heart! Onward, onward, it saith, and where beauty leads, there it follows. Whether it be the tinkle of a lone sheep bell o'er some quiet landscape, or the glimmer of beauty in sylvan places, or the show of soul in some passing eye, the heart knows and makes answer, following. . . . Know then, that for you is neither surfeit nor content. In your rocking chair, by your window dreaming, shall you long, alone. In your rocking chair, by your window, shall you dream such happiness as you may never feel.[5]

This is the compulsive quest, which brings with it both fleeting joy and the sad realization that one is yet separated from what is desired. It is a truth often expressed in literature, prominent in such diverse works as the *Tenth Satire* of Juvenal, Voltaire's *Candide*, and Dr. Johnson's

---

Senancour and Amiel), and that some of the most pronounced cases of apparently causeless melancholy are to be observed in optimistic, prosperous periods of history.

5 *Sister Carrie* (New York: Heritage, 1939), pp. 386-387.

Rasselas. It is at the very heart of Eugene O'Neill's *Beyond the Horizon.* In the opening scene Robert, who is to die at the end of the play, starts on a journey; he tries to make his brother see why he must go, in these words:

> Supposing I was to tell you that it's just Beauty that's calling me, the beauty of the far off and unknown, . . . the need of freedom of the great wide spaces, the joy of watching on and on—in quest of the secret which is hidden over there, beyond the horizon?[6]

A sense of separation from what is desired, a ceaseless longing which always points beyond—this then is the essence of the attitude I have attempted to describe.

The usual vocabulary of literary criticism and its usual methods of reference may suggest at first that in *Sehnsucht* we have not one but several attitudes. This depends upon the level at which we make our subdivision, in other words, what we are looking for. It is possible to delineate an attitude in literature in a number of ways, as the same room in a house, the dining room for example, may be thought of with a variety of associations. Food, companionship, beauty of surroundings, memories of holiday occasions—all these may be bound up with this room, and yet it is still only one place. It has a variety of mental associations, and yet these have a common basis: they are all connected with the same definite geographical location. *Sehnsucht* may be thought of as one of the rooms in the house of literature; it has a variety of "furnishings" and associations, but these are united in a common basis—a sense of displacement.

This "room" is naturally connected with other parts of the house, that is, other literary themes—fate, love, liberty, courage, etc. (such a neat classification of experience being problematical of course)—yet it may still be thought of as one unit. Thus *Sehnsucht* may be said to represent just as much a basic theme in literature as love, which appears under many definitions and in connection with various other themes, but still refers to a central idea.

6 *The Plays of Eugene O'Neill* (New York: Random House, 1946), III, 85.

The relation of Sehnsucht *to Romanticism*

If *Sehnsucht* is after all a basic concept in literature, the question immediately arises, Why has it been so long unseen or at least unnamed? The answer is simply that it has long been subsumed in something else, in that most nebulous "ism" of literary history, "Romanticism."
I hasten to add that Romanticism is called nebulous here not because it involves metaphysical concepts. The word is nebulous because it has been asked to include so many different tendencies. Arthur O. Lovejoy in an address before the Modern Language Association in 1923 suggested that a great deal of confusion in the history of ideas could be avoided if writers would be careful to discriminate among the *various* romanticisms.[7] He traced some of the differences in the romantic movements of Germany, England, and France, showing how the word has come to mean so many things that it has ceased to perform the function of a verbal sign. As he foresaw, the radical remedy for this situation—namely, that we should all stop talking about "Romanticism"—has not been adopted. Nor is it likely soon to be.

Beginning in the twenties there was a mild (and in a few quarters, a vehement) reaction against the poets of the English Romantic Movement. This reaction has continued to the present time, although there are now signs of a new respect for some of these writers.[8] Their decline in popularity at least among the avant-garde was due partly to the anti-romantic criticism of T. E. Hulme, T. S. Eliot, and Irving Babbitt. And two World Wars doubtless made any presupposition of the innate goodness of man less tenable, or any view of the world as the many-colored garment of God hard to maintain. The Romantic Movement has not been without its champions in our time, however, and

---

[7] "On the Discrimination of Romanticisms," *PMLA*, 39 (June, 1924), 229-253.

[8] John Bayley's *The Romantic Survival*, Frank Kermode's *The Romantic Image*, and R. A. Foakes' *The Romantic Assertion* are among the most recent revaluations of the English Romantic Movement.

there have been innumerable studies of the Romantic poets, many highly sympathetic. But it remains a controversial period, having enemies and admirers in a way that the Elizabethan or Medieval periods do not. The interesting fact for my purposes is that Romanticism continues to be written with a capital "r" and is still talked about as if it were one thing—often when it is under attack or when it is not fashionable to be a Romantic.

I agree with Lovejoy's recommendation that we try to discriminate among romanticisms when we refer to particular writers. This, however, does not mean that we can easily dispense with the capital "r." Romanticism seems to be a genus which contains many species. The very fact that the word apparently cannot be stamped out indicates that it may refer to a complex of ideas for which we need a word. (It is admittedly a vague term, but do not the semanticists teach us that every language has useful and meaningful vaguenesses?) This complex of ideas no doubt contains diverse and apparently unrelated elements: a delight in the marvelous, egoism, soaring aspiration, an enthusiastic sensibility to the beauties of nature, etc. The question arises, Is there any common denominator in all these ideas?

Of course it is difficult to find such a denominator if one considers such things as Gothic novels, medievalism, valentines, and revolutionary politics to be authentic manifestations of Romanticism. But if it be understood not as a particular kind of material but as a state of mind, these things will be seen as phenomena which make use of certain Romantic machinery without necessarily expressing the essential attitude.[9] When the more superficial aspects are pruned away, the following might be listed as the chief characteristics of the Romantic temper:

1. An emphasis on emotion rather than reason, the heart opposed to the head (this idea having been set forth by George Sand, Cazamian, Thrall, and Hibbard).

[9] I am indebted to Professor Nathan Starr in my understanding of Romanticism here. He has called such things as valentines and Gothicism only "frosting on the cake."

2. A desire to find the infinite within the finite (Fairchild).

3. A liberation of the less conscious levels of the mind; an intoxicated dreaming (Lucas).

4. A revival of the sense of wonder (Watts-Dunton).

5. Vague aspiration (Phelps).[10]

Common to all these definitions is the element of aspiration and longing for what we may call, for want of a better word, the infinite—that which transcends everyday finite experience. It is this, I believe, which contrasts the Romantic attitude with the Classical. The Classical spirit in literature is not concerned with "aspirations towards the infinite," with "high soaring and deep diving," in the words of T. E. Hulme. The Classical spirit calls for preciseness in form; it endeavors to say "what oft was thought, but ne'er so well express'd"; it seeks a zestful accuracy of language and, as Eliot has put it, a "unified sensibility" which submits the creative process at every stage to a self-conscious intellectual mastery.

It is not a question of which attitude is the correct one. We cannot have enduring literature without some of both. Even the ethereal Shelley, whose work has invited so much attack in our time, is preoccupied with achieving the right sort of formal effects for his "message," especially in metrics.[11] And the most rabid anti-romantic has his immortal longings and "vague" sense of aspiration. Thus I see the two attitudes as not ultimately opposed but complementary. The Romantic attitude represents always an unusually vigorous reaction to the world; this reaction may reflect acceptance or rejection of one's environment but it must be intense. It is here that the common denominator,

[10] See Ernest Bernbaum, *Guide Through the Romantic Movement*, Second Edition (New York: Ronald, 1949), pp. 301-302 and pp. 315-317 for a fuller summary of definitions and bibliographical information concerning the sources cited here.

[11] I am thinking of such things as Shelley's experimentation with anapestic and spondaic measure, his striving for a proper Hellenic tone in the formal effects of *Prometheus Unbound* and *The Cenci*, his careful use of the various elegiac conventions in *Adonais*, and the deliberate development of "Ode to the West Wind."

a sense of aspiration and longing for the infinite, comes in. When the reaction is an exuberant "Yea" to environment, we have the Romantic's traditional love of nature and sense of oneness with it. When the reaction is a vehement "Nay," we have tales of the land of faerie, dreams of better times in the past or in the future, or an attempt to invest with wonder the everyday and the commonplace.

Without the Classical temper to order and render articulate visions of things well nigh ineffable, the author could never share them with anyone else. Or he might express these visions in such loose, disjointed form that our aesthetic sense would cause us to reject them. On the other hand, without the Romantic temper man loses his unique gift for reacting imaginatively to his environment in all its fullness. The Neo-classical ideal of submitting everything to reason leaves much of experience unaccounted for. Without a groping for answers, even when such answers cannot be stated clearly, without an openness to experience in all its inexplicable variety and strangeness, art dies.

I have been interested in exploring the nature of Romanticism for the light it may shed on *Sehnsucht* as a theme in literature. Whether or not the reader sees in Romanticism the "common denominator" which I find there, it will be clear how I am using the term. And it will be seen that there is a definite similarity between Romanticism as I have described it and the particular attitude which is characterized by a sense of separation from what is desired, a ceaseless longing which points always beyond. It will be seen that *Sehnsucht* indeed represents an aspect of that larger "ism" which has been explained as a vigorous reaction for or against one's environment, resulting in feelings of wonder and aspiration. One might argue that wherever we find the Romantic attitude in its most intense forms, we may very well find *Sehnsucht*. But accepting its omnipresence in Romanticism is not necessary to seeing a relation between *Sehnsucht* and the Romantic temper. It will be enough if the reader can see here an explanation for the fact that the attitude has gone long unnamed and undefined, namely, because it was subsumed under Romanticism to which it bears a close relation.

The origin of Sehnsucht

To account for the origin of a part of something, it is logical to look to the origin of the whole. There have been numerous attempts to trace the paternity of the larger complex of ideas to which *Sehnsucht* belongs. Bernbaum and Lovejoy, with tongue in cheek, have listed various nominees for the title "The Founder of Romanticism."[12] These include such diverse literary and philosophical figures as Kant, Rousseau, St. Paul, Plato, and Homer. Though any search for such an originator is bound to be inconclusive if not entirely pointless, one might argue quite cogently that if writers dating as far back as the ancient Greeks show signs of the Romantic approach, it is evident that Romanticism has been with us for a long time.

As a reaction to environment which results in a sense of wonder and aspiration, it could be considered as old as recorded history in the Western world. (And though I know Eastern literature only in translation, I believe it would be safe to say that Romanticism is not alien to the Orient.) Behind "causeless" melancholy, a fear of the numinous, and the perennial searching instinct—whether it be for the Blue Flower, the Blue Bird, or the Well at the World's End—we find the underlying sense of estrangement Lewis has called *Sehnsucht*. If the larger attitude, Romanticism, is fundamental in the experience at least of Western man, then *Sehnsucht*, representing an aspect of the Romantic attitude, may be said to be fundamental also.

If one is doubtful of the survival power of the *Sehnsucht* archetype, he has only to look at such recent novels as Saul Bellow's *Mr. Sammler's Planet*, the plays of Christopher Fry or Tennessee Williams, or the poetry of Dylan Thomas, Wallace Stevens, and W. H. Auden. Quotations from authors like these would point up Simone Weil's poignant summary of the archetype in *Waiting for God:*

> When we possess a beautiful thing, we still desire something. We do not in the least know what it is. We want to get behind the

---

[12] See Lovejoy's *PMLA* article and Bernbaum's *Guide,* pp. 302-303.

beauty, but it ... like a mirror sends back our own desire for
goodness. It is a ... mystery that is painfully tantalizing.[13]

To be sure, this kind of longing seems more pronounced
in some periods than in others. Particularly intriguing is
the fact that *Sehnsucht* in literature seems definitely to
have increased since the Romantic movements of France,
Germany, and England. Whether or not this is related to
the "dissociation of sensibility" which Eliot says occurred
in the late seventeenth century I cannot attempt to say.
Changes in artistic sensibility are closely bound up with
changes in the philosophical climate. And the generations
which have lived since Descartes and Kant, since the rise of
industrialism and specialization, Darwinism and the New
Psychology have had to face problems which no prior
period faced. To prove that *Sehnsucht* in literature has
increased with the increasing complexity and rootlessness
of modern life would probably be statistically impossible.
Yet when one reads through an anthology of Western
literature, he is very likely to get the impression that our
scientific age is beset by longings which seem bizarre and
incongruous beside the sanity and poise of earlier periods.
Whatever its origin or the factors contributing to its
apparent increase, *Sehnsucht* is a prevalent theme in literature. It cannot, I believe, be wholly accounted for on
historical, social, or psychological grounds. It is simply a
"given" of experience and when studied as such may shed
some light on literature and the nature of man as well.
Because I am indebted chiefly to C. S. Lewis for my
understanding of *Sehnsucht*, I turn now to the subject of
his development as an author and thinker.

13 *Waiting for God*, translated by Emma Crawford (New York: Putnam's,
1951), p. 165.

II LEWIS' EARLY DEVELOPMENT: The Search for "Joy"

Somewhat . . . the soul seeketh, and what that is directly it knoweth not, yet very intentive desire thereof doth so incite it, that all other known delights and pleasures are laid aside, they give place to the search of this but only suspected desire.

—Richard Hooker

Every philosophy, according to Nietzsche, is a species of unconscious biography. The same may be said, with perhaps a similar degree of exaggeration, of aesthetic theories, and in particular of Lewis' concept of *Sehnsucht*. One cannot understand the importance he gives to this concept without knowing of the search upon which his mind and imagination were bent for many years.

There are of course dangers in the biographical approach to literature. Lewis himself has discussed these dangers in *The Personal Heresy.*[1] Yet in my mind Lewis' share in that work stands as a somewhat overstated corrective to the biographical-psychological preoccupation of so much nineteenth-century criticism. For nothing he has ever written is impersonal. His books have the same force of personality which we find in those of G. B. Shaw or Dr. Johnson.

---

[1] This was written in controversy with E. M. W. Tillyard, first in *Essays and Studies by Members of the English Association*, appearing later as *The Personal Heresy: a Controversy* (London: Oxford, 1939).

And he is far too shrewd to suppose that the self is ever screened out in any literary work, no matter how professedly detached or how filled with pseudo-scientific constructions.

Moreover, in this study I am not simply interested in interpreting Lewis' work. This is an attempt to explore an idea, to discover how that idea finds expression in Lewis' writing, and to examine the validity of that idea as an instrument of literary analysis.

What manner of man

From 1955 to 1963 Lewis held the chair of Medieval and Renaissance Literature at Cambridge. For the previous thirty years he was tutor and fellow in English at Magdalen College, Oxford. Yet he was no rigid specialist, confining his conversation to literature and the state of the weather. He ranged over the fenced enclosures of modern departmentalized knowledge with amazing accuracy and a powerful memory. Kenneth Tynan, who studied under Lewis at Oxford, says that Lewis had "more knowledge at his finger-tips" than anyone he has ever known, "and probably more than anyone else who has appeared on the cover of *Time* magazine."[2] In the cited issue of *Time* (Sept. 8, 1947) Lewis' lectures were described as unusual in that often there was standing room only. Tynan says that Lewis "revivified" the Middle Ages for numberless Oxford undergraduates "by presenting medieval studies as a controversial topic for immediate debate, on which the closure has not yet been forced."[3]

His lectures were enthusiastically received also because he talked well, with vitality and gusto. His personality, in fact, seems to have been just the opposite of the one suggested by the picture which appeared in the earlier books published in this country— a dead-pan likeness which

2 Cecil Beaton and Kenneth Tynan, *Persona Grata* (London: Putnam, 1954), p. 69. This is a collection of sketches of well-known contemporaries; there are photographs by Beaton and a running text by Tynan.

3 *Ibid.*, p. 69.

prepared one interviewer for a dour and forbidding personality. The interviewer was pleasantly surprised to find the man "in the flesh . . . alive and aglow like his books."[4] Kenneth Tynan said Lewis combined the manner of Friar Tuck with the mind of St. Augustine.

Amiability, however, did not prevent Lewis from engaging in that favorite sport of dons, "applying the elenchus." Dom Bede Griffiths in his autobiography *The Golden String* says that he discovered in Lewis "the most exact and penetrating mind" he had ever encountered.[5] Tynan adds that at the end of an hour's session, Lewis would inquire "in a voice juicy and measured whether the student feels any 'new acquist of true experience from this great event.' " If the pupil's response is merely a compliment, he is displeased. " 'Keep a strict eye,' he will say, 'on eulogistic and dyslogistic adjectives. They should *diagnose*—not merely blame—and *distinguish*—not merely praise.' "[6]

Lewis' success as writer has been no less remarkable than his success as teacher. He has at least four separate groups of readers: the scholarly audience who regard his *Allegory of Love, Preface to Paradise Lost*, and his book on sixteenth-century English literature as basic literary studies; the readers of his "popular" theological and philosophical works, these having been well received by a variety of critics—among them, Christopher Morley, W. H. Auden, Charles Hartshorne, and Etienne Gilson. Third, the lovers of "fantastic" fiction for whom Lewis' interplanetary trilogy and his *Till We Have Faces* are special things of their kind. And fourth, he has an ever increasing audience as a writer of children's stories. *The Last Battle* of his Narnia series won him the Carnegie Medal for the best children's book published in 1956, and Roger Lancelyn Green, an authority on juvenile fiction, places Lewis with the half dozen best writers for children in this century.[7]

[4] David Wesley Soper, "An Interview with C. S. Lewis," *Zion's Herald,* Jan. 14, 1948, p. 28.

[5] Dom Bede Griffiths, *The Golden String* (New York: P. J. Kenedy, 1954), p. 44.

[6] *Persona Grata*, p. 69.

[7] *Tellers of Tales* (London: British Book Centre, 1954), pp. 259-260.

One cannot help wondering how such a versatile writer, of hearty disposition and a strong rationalistic bent as well, ever became preoccupied with *Sehnsucht*. Fortunately, this is a case where biography lights up rather than obscures an author's work.

There are several main sources for knowledge of Lewis' life and background. The first of these is a study by Chad Walsh called *C. S. Lewis: Apostle to the Skeptics.* Published in 1949, this book introduced Lewis as a personality to many who knew him only as the author of one book, assigned to this or that pigeonhole. It not only humanized Lewis for readers frightened a little by the passport likeness in his early books and by a certain amount of crotchety dogmatism in those books, but it did something else. Walsh skillfully laid out, for lay readers, some of the main roads and by-paths of Lewis' philosophy. And one of the things which he saw was Lewis' continuing interest in romantic longing, an aspect of his thought which has received little attention since he is so generally regarded as rationalistic or Neo-Thomist in outlook.

Then in 1955 Lewis published *Surprised by Joy,* an autobiography of his first thirty years. (This work read in conjunction with Lewis' early allegory, *The Pilgrim's Regress*, reveals *Sehnsucht* as a theme with contrapuntal variations throughout Lewis' development.) And beginning with Clyde Kilby's *The Christian World of C. S. Lewis* there have been a number of more recent studies, among which the most important are those edited or written by Lewis' literary executor, Walter Hooper. Hooper and Roger Lancelyn Green are doing a biography of Lewis which is to be published in 1974. With the guidance particularly of *The Pilgrim's Regress* and *Surprised by Joy,* I turn now to a consideration of Lewis' early life, which will follow his awareness of *Sehnsucht* up to his late twenties, when he underwent an experience which was to alter all his future interpretations of that "sense of separation from what is desired, that longing which always points beyond."[8]

[8] My definition of *Sehnsucht* from p. 23.

Childhood in Ireland

Lewis says in the preface to *Surprised by Joy* that he knows of no autobiography in which the parts devoted to the earlier years are not by far the most interesting.[9] Of course by "earlier years" he means more than Freud's "first five." *Surprised by Joy* is subtitled "The Shape of My Early Life," and Lewis explains that in the first half of the book he is going to spread the net pretty wide in order that the reader may understand what sort of person his childhood and adolescence have made him. The second half is devoted to tracing his adult intellectual interests and particularly to recounting the thought processes which led him in his thirtieth year to a kind of conversion experience.

It is, as Lewis acknowledges in the Preface, a "suffocatingly subjective" book, and this self-conscious book is a "sport of nature" so far as Lewis' work is concerned. For a writer generally less self-conscious is hard to imagine. Yet the subject of *Surprised by Joy* is the subject of this chapter and I must therefore deal in detail with what it reveals of Lewis' development.

Born in 1898, Lewis describes his early childhood as happy. His father was a reasonably prosperous solicitor in Belfast, his mother a sunny and tranquil person. Indeed their temperaments seemed to balance one another. Lewis reflects that his father, who was descended from a Welsh farmer, was like all true Welshmen "sentimental, passionate, and rhetorical, easily moved both to anger and to tenderness." His mother's family, the Hamiltons, were "a cooler race." "Their minds were critical and ironic and they had the talent for happiness in a high degree—went straight for it as experienced travelers go for the best seat in a train" (*Surprised by Joy*, p. 3). Both parents were by the standards of northern Ireland in the early 1900's moderately cultured people. His mother was a B. A. of Queen's College, Belfast, and before Lewis was eight, she had started him in both French and Latin. His father was

9 New York: Harcourt, Brace, 1956, preface.

fond of the sort of poetry that has plenty of rhetoric and pathos and greatly enjoyed all humorous authors, from Dickens to W. W. Jacobs. He was a fine *raconteur* himself and was never happier than when exchanging "wheezes," as anecdotes were called in the Lewis family (p. 5). Neither parent was a lover of Romantic literature. Lewis says there was no copy of Keats or Shelley in their house and the copy of Coleridge was never opened.

Lewis and his brother Warren, older by three years, enjoyed a big house, good food, a good "nanny," and a garden. But neither of their parents had ever listened for "the horns of elfland" and it was entirely on their own that Warren and Clive discovered the far away and long ago—or more appropriately, "never-never" lands of their own imagining. They drew and they wrote stories about knights in armor, India, and "dressed mice." And Lewis discovered what he recalled later as the first beauty he ever knew when his brother brought into the nursery the lid of a biscuit tin which he had covered with moss and decorated with twigs and flowers, making it a toy garden or a toy forest. "What the real garden had failed to do, the toy garden did. It made me aware of nature, not, indeed as a storehouse of forms and colors but as something cool, dewy, fresh, exuberant." Then he adds, significantly: "I do not think the impression was very important at the moment, but it soon became important in memory. As long as I live my imagination of Paradise will retain something of my brother's toy garden" (p. 7).

Another and similar aesthetic experience was permanently to affect Lewis' imagination. From the nursery windows he would drink in the view of the Castlereagh Hills, which though not very far off, seemed then altogether unattainable. "The Green Hills," as he called them, taught him longing, made him, "for good or ill," before he was six years old, "a votary of the Blue Flower" (p. 7).

When Lewis was seven his brother was sent away to an English boarding school and Lewis' life, except for his parents and governess, became increasingly one of solitude. He began writing a history of "Animal-Land" and even made maps of it. In chronicling Animal-Land, however, he was not engaging in the fantasies of lazy reverie. He was so utterly businesslike about it that, in retrospect, he considered it valuable preparation for the craft of novel-writing. (According to Walter Hooper, one discovers in Lewis' juvenilia a surprising interest in politics. It does not seem so odd then that during the War, when English enrollments were down at Oxford, Lewis chose to teach courses in political theory.)

In the period between ages six and eight he read *Gulliver, A Connecticut Yankee in King Arthur's Court*, and a children's trilogy by E. Nesbit. But he says it was not until the Beatrix Potter stories that he discovered beauty in books. He returned again and again to *Squirrel Nutkin* to reawaken something which "troubled" him with a poignant delight, the "Idea of Autumn" (*Surprised by Joy*, p. 16). He was to experience the same troubling joy in a translation of Tegner's *Drapa.* He recalls the day when he idly turned its pages for the first time, his eyes lighting upon:

> I heard a voice that cried,
> Balder the beautiful
> Is dead, is dead—

He felt at once "uplifted into the huge regions of northern sky," desiring with an almost sickening intensity something "cold, spacious, severe, pale, and remote" (p. 17).

For purposes of this study, the chronology here is important. Lewis says that he experienced *Sehnsucht* before he was six years old. This was four years before the first traumatic experience of his life, the gradual death of his mother from cancer. This sorrow separated Lewis and his brother from their father—under the pressure of anxiety he became bad-tempered and unjust, and for a time the boys found comfort only in their reliance on each other. The glimpses of "Joy" in Beatrix Potter, the "toy garden," and "the Green Hills" belong to the comfortable, happy years—before the sudden loss of support he was to experience in his mother's death.

In fact, the usual psychological explanation will not do at all here. Although Lewis sees his mother's death as the

end of "settled happiness," and although it may very well
have intensified *Sehnsucht,* Lewis gives a more likely key
when later in the book he seeks to account for the sources
of his early "pessimism." He says that early in life he had
met with "a great dismay" in discovering that he had
inherited from his father a small physical defect which was
to shape in some measure his interests and influence his
temperament. As a boy he discovered that having only one
joint in the thumb made him exceedingly awkward at
games, and this awkwardness was later to contribute to a
social reticence.

Lewis himself does not trace his preoccupation with
Sehnsucht to this defect. He simply says that this clumsi-
ness, coupled with his father's exaggerated talk of being on
the verge of going to the poorhouse and the necessity of
"work-work-work till you die," early bred in him a disposition to look upon life with pessimism (*Surprised by
Joy,* pp. 63-65). Yet, if those who believe that all roads
lead to Freud would account for Lewis' *Sehnsucht* as mere
compensation for this unhappy outlook, they can do so
only by ignoring the nature of the complex of emotions
and ideas to which Lewis has given this name.

Early schools

When Lewis was ten his father decided that it was time for
him to be sent off to school in England. As the correspon-
dence shows, the elder Lewis looked carefully into a number of schools and then, after thoughtful deliberation,
selected probably the very worst one of all. Located in
Hertfordshire, the Wynyard school is called "Belsen" in
Lewis' autobiography. It was financially and academically
on its last legs, with an insane headmaster and only a
dozen pupils. Both Lewis and his brother went there in the
fall of 1908, and though they were beaten, half-starved,
and taught little but geometry, their father continued to
see "Oldie," the headmaster, and the already defunct
school through the eyes of one who had read Oldie's
prospectus and composed "a school story in his own
mind" (p. 30). Unfortunately, when the boys were home

on vacation they told very little of what they might have, partly because communication with their father was not easy and partly because they did not want to admit their fear of Oldie. Thus Lewis spent two years at Belsen, a grim period.

Yet in retrospect, Lewis found that there was something good in his experience at Oldie's. It was there that he first responded to the liturgy of the Anglican Church. Oldie's pupils were taken to church twice on Sundays, and though Lewis believes there was in these services no unnecessary preoccupation with fear of the divine holiness, the thought of Hell loomed large in his boyhood mind. He had been born into a Church of Ireland home, but he says in connection with Belsen:

> If in my books I have spoken too much of Hell, and if critics want a historical explanation of that fact, they must seek it not in the supposed Puritanism of my Ulster childhood but in the Anglo-Catholicism of the church at Belsen. I feared for my soul; especially on certain blazing moonlit nights in that curtainless dormitory—how the sound of other boys breathing in their sleep comes back! (p. 34)

The effect, he thinks now, was strangely good. He began to be seriously interested in religion and to attempt to obey his conscience.

One sees a reflection of this boyhood sense of the numinous in the first chapter of Lewis' early book, *The Pilgrim's Regress: An Allegorical Apology for Christianity, Reason, and Romanticism.* The argument for Book I begins:

> A boy brought up from childhood to fear God more than to love Him, and to fear Hell more than God, thereby learns at last to acknowledge duties which he cannot perform and to remember death. All unconscious with this teaching are the fits of strange Desire, which haunt him from his earliest years, for something which cannot be named; something which he can describe only as "Not this," "Far farther," or "Yonder."[10]

10 *The Pilgrim's Regress: An Allegorical Apology for Christianity, Reason, and Romanticism* (London: Sheed and Ward, 1933), p. 11. A revised edition

These "fits of strange Desire" which come unexpectedly, awakening an almost painfully happy nostalgia for something "other and outer," Lewis has spoken of as both *Sehnsucht* and "Joy." It is interesting that at Oldie's, "Joy," in Lewis' special sense of the word, was "not only absent but forgotten" (*Surprised by Joy*, p. 34). If it were chiefly an escape mechanism, one would expect it to have been frequently experienced at Belsen, where vacations were longed for as the sick await recovery or prisoners the day of liberation. Each holiday at home seemed to be very Heaven, marred only by the fact that it was temporary. Thoughts of returning to school were suppressed until the very last moment when there could be no doubt that vacation was indeed over. The evening drive to the quay on the Irish sea seemed always the end of the world, and yet, as he gradually learned, vacation *would* come again.

> In all seriousness I think that the life of faith is easier to me because of these memories. To think, in sunny and confident times, that I shall die and rot, or to think that one day all this universe will slip away and become a memory (as Oldie slipped away into memory three times a year, and with him the canes and the disgusting food, the stinking sanitation and the cold beds)—this is easier to us if we have seen just that sort of thing happening before. We have learned not to take things at their face value. (p. 37)

The absence of "Joy" at Belsen was probably connected with the decline in imaginative life which Lewis underwent there. His reading was mostly "twaddling school stories . . . mere wish fulfilment and fantasy; one enjoyed vicariously the triumphs of the hero" (p. 35). Happily for his intellectual development, the school "sank unlamented" in the summer of 1910, and after one term at a boarding school near Belfast, he was sent off at the age of thirteen to what he calls "Chartres," actually Cherbourg House, a preparatory school connected with Malvern College. His brother attended the college.

---

has been published by Geoffrey Bles (London, 1943) and by Wm. B. Eerdmans (Grand Rapids, 1958).

The young atheist

It was at this school that Lewis slowly became a defiant atheist. He sees three main reasons for his rejection of theism (a vital Christianity never having been very fully a part of his experience). There was at Chartres a kind and motherly matron floundering in the mazes of Theosophy and Spiritualism, who "little by little, unconsciously, unintentionally . . . blunted all the sharp edges" of his belief in God. The moonlit nights in the dormitory at Belsen faded away and he passed into "the cool evening of Higher Thought, where there was nothing to be obeyed, and nothing to be believed except what was either comforting or exciting" (p. 60). In rejecting the idea of a personal God, he felt himself tremendously relieved of a heavy burden. This was the duty of prayer, in which through misunderstanding he had failed utterly, for as a boy he believed that by sheer effort of the will he could drum up a realization of the presence of God.

His growing acquaintance with the classics also encouraged his atheism, for, he reasoned, if the pagan gods were merely myths, the Christian God was probably a myth also. But most potent in his rejection of theism was what he has called the "Argument from Undesign"—in Lucretius' words:

> Had God designed the world, it would not be
> A world so frail and faulty as we see.[11]

While a thirteen-year-old's ideas of Undesign may be somewhat naive and too highly personal, they are no less convincing to him. Lewis' reading in H. G. Wells and Sir Robert Ball had impressed upon him "the vastness and cold of space, the littleness of Man," and his own sensitivity to the sufferings of unfortunates like the beggar at the school gate had led him to accept atheism as the only position possible to a thinking person.

In *The Pilgrim's Regress* there are hints of autobiography in this connection. The boy John is unable to find any

11 Quoted in *Surprised by Joy*, p. 65.

comfort or meaning in religion. He is repelled by ecclesiastical solemnity and artificiality and in the face of his first experience with death (that of his uncle), he is shocked and sickened by conventional attitudes (pp. 25-27). In telling of his mother's death in *Surprised by Joy,* Lewis comments that he will never know what is meant when dead bodies are called beautiful. Death is hideous terror to a child, and "all the fuss and flummery" of the funeral whereby adults try to cover up its ugliness early bred in him a distaste "for all that is public, all that belongs to the collective" (p. 20).

It was during his time at Chartres that Lewis began again to experience that peculiar thing he called "Joy." The years at the two previous boarding schools he later regarded as a kind of long winter, a period between childhood and adolescence (ages ten through thirteen), when the imagination was sleeping. In *Surprised by Joy,* he recalls when this winter at last broke up, fairly early in his time at Chartres. Sitting in one of the schoolrooms, he picked up a literary periodical, perhaps *The Bookman* or *The Times Literary Supplement,* and discovered one of Arthur Rackham's illustrations for *Siegfried and the Twilight of the Gods.* The scene and the sound of the title were enough to engulf him in "Northernness," as he had once been so seemingly long ago in Tegner's *Drapa.* He knew at once ". . . that Siegfried (whatever it might be) belonged to the same world as Balder and the sun-ward sailing cranes. And with that plunge . . . there arose at once, almost like heartbreak, the memory of Joy itself" (p. 73).

The far-off northern twilight and the pangs of Joy remembered from childhood (the Castlereagh Hills, his brother's toy garden) "flowed together into a single, unendurable sense of desire and loss, which suddenly became one with the loss of the whole experience" (p. 76).

This incident led to an avid collecting of information on Wagnerian opera, to a reading of all the Norse mythology he could get hold of, to writing poems about Mime, Sieglinde, and Fafner. He recalls cycling among the Wicklow Mountains during a school holiday and looking for scenes which might belong to the Wagnerian world. And soon (he cannot remember exactly when) Nature itself began to give the pang of Joy. What had largely been communicated through books began now to come to him in Nature as Wordsworth saw it. He developed the habit of surrendering himself to the mood of a particular scene, tasting with skin and nose and eyes (p. 78).

Lewis believed that there was an erotic element in his response to "Northernness." But it was not a cheap or morbid eroticism. In fact, it had a much more "romantic" quality about it than did his earliest responses to feminine charms. He reflects that the dancing mistress at Chartres was the first woman he ever looked upon as physically desirable. But what he felt for her was not romantic passion but "sheer appetite; the prose and not the poetry of the Flesh" (p. 69). The latter came to him more nearly in "the Northernness," which seemed indeed more important than anything else—even his religious difficulties—because it conveyed Joy. His interest in religion, he says, was overshadowed by Northernness partly because it contained elements which his religion ought to have contained and did not. Northernness had a quality of aesthetic exaltation about it which Lewis had not found in Christianity and which he was seeking in the occult. Where religion had failed, Wagner and Norse mythology were able to awaken that strange excitement which at times he had experienced in his childhood. Thus it was that his imagination was early bent toward the Germanic while his Celtic origins had little direct effect upon him.[12]

"Preparation for Public Life" at Wyvern

When Lewis moved up from Chartres to Wyvern (actually Malvern College), he was somewhat dazzled at first. At Chartres the boys had lived under the shadow of "the Coll," and the Wyvernian athletes and prefects, who were

[12] That Lewis himself realizes the dominance of Germanic influence upon him is reflected in a comment he made to Chad Walsh. See C. S. Lewis: Apostle to the Skeptics (New York: Macmillan, 1949), pp. 2-3.

called Bloods, embodied all that was most worthy in life. But Lewis was soon to become deeply disillusioned with Bloodery and with British private schools in general. His acute unhappiness and fatigue under the fagging system and his ineptitude at games no doubt prejudiced him against the whole business quite apart from its intrinsic faults. But on looking back, his judgment, tempered by time, remained a stern one. He wonders if the predominance in England for the last thirty years of "a bitter, truculent, skeptical, debunking, and cynical intelligentsia" does not owe something to the private schools. Such education was to be a "Preparation for Public Life," that those trained in such institutions might be ready to bear "the white man's burden" among the lesser races of the world. Lewis speculates that the fagging system has often produced "retaliatory pride and contempt," for "no one is more likely to be arrogant than a lately freed slave" (*Surprised by Joy*, p. 107).

The social struggle dominated every aspect of school life (games, clothes, friends, amusements, and vices) and made the Wyvernians the "least spontaneous" society Lewis ever knew. For that reason the elaborate pederastic courtships of each house, though offensive to him at the time and, since he was one of the youngest boys, "opaque" to his imagination, provided the one "counterpoise" to the social struggle.

A perversion was the only chink left through which something spontaneous and uncalculated could creep in. Plato was right after all. Eros, turned upside down, blackened, distorted, and filthy, still bore the traces of his divinity. (*Surprised by Joy*, p. 110)

In discussing life at Malvern College, Lewis says that for the remainder of his autobiography he must tell two separate stories—a second one being required to describe his imaginative life as it related to Joy. Previously his outer life and the fleeting experiences of Joy had seemed to belong to the same story, to have some unity. (One is tempted to ask: Is there something inherent in the structures of "mature" society which forces them apart? Lewis was not the first to experience the division. Wordsworth and Walter Pater tell of a similar discovery.)

Of his imaginative life at this prep school, only a part of which was concerned with Joy, we learn that Lewis discovered there a deep enthusiasm for Horace's odes, the *Aeneid,* and Euripides' *Bacchae.* Especially in the latter he tasted a new mythology quite different from the world of Loki, Odin, and Wagnerian opera. A new quality had entered his imagination—"something Mediterranean and volcanic" (*Surprised by Joy,* p. 113), something which I take to be rebellious and Shelleyan; he owns that it may have been unconsciously tied up with his dislike of Malvern.

Lewis was particularly fortunate in his Latin and Greek teacher, "Smewgy," as he was called. It was he who first taught Lewis the "right sensuality" of poetry, "how it should be savored and mouthed in solitude. Of Milton's 'Thrones, Dominations, Princedoms, Virtues, Powers' he said, 'That line made me happy for a week.' " And though Smewgy could enthrall with his reading of verse ("something midway between speech and song"), he could analyze a phrase in the text so exactly that Lewis began to see why accuracy is a necessary part of the sensibility one must bring to literature (pp. 111-112).

The other great blessing of Wyvern was the library. There one was "unfaggable" and might spend the whole lazy afternoon amid books and leisurely silence. Lewis revelled in his discovery of Yeats, Milton, and Celtic mythology, there being moments in his reading when he felt too happy to speak. Nature as well continued to exhilarate him as it had at Chartres:

> The mere smells were enough to make a man tipsy—cut grass, dew-dabbled mosses . . . wood burning . . . salt water. The senses ached. I was sick with desire; that sickness being better than health. (p. 118)

But all of this was separate from the sordid banalities, the hectic struggle of the Coll. In speaking of his final months there, Lewis expresses his regret at never having been able to adapt as well as his brother had, especially to games. This continued loneliness because he was to games as "the ass to the harp" (p. 130) naturally increased his absorption in the world of books. Very few boys of his age would have read so much or so deeply as Lewis had by the time he left Malvern in the summer of 1914. He was then more than ready to begin with a private tutor in preparation for the university.

"The Great Knock" and another frontier

Wyvern's "Smewgy" had started Lewis in Grammar and Rhetoric (in the medieval sense of these terms) and it was "Kirk"—or "The Great Knock," as his father called him—who was to teach Lewis Dialectic. Kirk was the former headmaster of Lurgan College who now lived in semi-retirement in Bookham, Surrey. A few weeks before his sixteenth birthday, Lewis came to live with the Kirkpatricks, and he had hardly arrived when the tall, lean Ulster Scotsman began picking apart his most casual comments. Kirk intended that no pupil of his should talk "nonsense" and he pursued every word the boy spoke, looking for inconsistencies in vocabulary, hasty generalizations, and other logical fallacies.

Though some students would have been offended by such constant vigilance, to Lewis it was "red beef and strong beer" (*Surprised by Joy*, p. 136). This was not the inane sort of grown-up conversation he had always detested, the endless batting around of ephemeral, inconsequential interests. Kirk's ruthless dialectic made it necessary for talk to be really about something, made it possible for one to feel, in conversation, uncommonly alive.

With virtually no preliminaries, he and his tutor plunged into Homer. They read not only the *Iliad* and the *Odyssey* but the Greek dramatists and Lucretius, Catullus, Tacitus, Herodotus, and Virgil—all in the original. Later Kirk branched out into German and Italian, using always the same method. After the briefest introduction with grammars and exercises, they opened to the first page of *Faust* or the *Inferno* and began to read. And Lewis' study of French with Mrs. Kirkpatrick took on a similar pattern.

His free-time reading during this period consisted chiefly of medieval literature or books which dealt with the Arthurian legend: Spenser, Malory, the *High History of the Holy Grail*, Chenier, Ronsard, *Gawain and the Green Knight*, and nearly all of William Morris.

Lewis observes in *Surprised by Joy* that had he been able to please himself he would always have lived as he did at Kirk's: to breakfast at eight and read or write till one, to finish lunch by two and then be off on a ramble over the countryside, returning by four to have tea in solitude, often with book in hand. Then to be at work again till the evening meal at seven and after that have time for talk with friends or for light reading. He reflects, however, that it was for his good that he was never able to lead for long at a time this "settled, calm, Epicurean life," for it is a life almost entirely selfish (*Surprised by Joy,* p. 143).

It is easy to see in the portrait of Mr. Sensible in *The Pilgrim's Regress* what Lewis means by this. Mr. Sensible is not well-to-do but he has a servant Drudge who ministers to his every need so that the days are left free for philosophy and the arts, for following a " 'common-sense' ideal of cultured, humane, and enlightened hedonism" (p. 87). This ideal has no room, however, for haunting Desire, except as it tickles certain feelings, and the religious impulse is something to be tasted rather than obeyed. Mr. Sensible feels that philosophy should be a mistress, not a master, as he explains to John: "Sense is easy. Reason is hard. Sense knows where to stop with gracious inconsistency, while Reason slavishly follows an abstract logic whither she knows not" (p. 86).

Mr. Sensible is impressive in his urbanity, his wit and learning—in the array of Greek, Latin, and French quotations he tosses confidently about (several of which he misinterprets or misquotes in his disdain of pedantic accuracy). But his whole life collapses one morning when he awakes to find Drudge has left him.

It is the ultimate unreasonableness of this kind of life, together with its dependence on good health and the hard work of other people, which caused Lewis to attack it in his earlier book. That he could do so with such insight bears out what he says in *Surprised by Joy* of knowing its temptations first-hand.

Kirk's rationalism taught Lewis respect for reason. Yet by the time Lewis wrote *The Pilgrim's Regress* (1933) he had discovered that rationalism, if followed closely, could give no more significance to fleeting pangs of Joy than did Mr. Sensible's philosophy. Although Lewis acknowledges his great debt to Kirk, there may be just a little of that tenacious logician in the portrait of Mr. Enlightenment, another false guide in the *Regress*. Kirk was a rationalist "of the old, high and dry nineteenth-century type" (*Surprised by Joy*, p. 139), and he considered atheism in religion as inevitable for any honest seeker after truth. Like Mr. Enlightenment, he was strong on anthropology. Yet Lewis, unlike the young man in the allegory who is beguiled into rejecting his religion, says that he cannot blame his youthful atheism on Kirk. What he discovered in his tutor's logic was "merely fresh ammunition for a position already chosen" (p. 140).

During this period of Lewis' life he had the good fortune to have one close friend his own age who shared many of his interests. This was a neighbor boy in Belfast whom he had ignored so long as Warren was at home, but now that his brother was away in the army, vacations would have been exceedingly lonely had it not been for Arthur Greeves. Their friendship was strong from the moment Lewis accidentally saw him reading *Myths of the Norsemen* and discovered that he too had felt that stab of Joy which came out of the North. With Arthur he also discovered a liking for the novels of Scott, Austen, and the Brontës. These provided "an admirable complement" to Lewis' more fantastic reading and "each was the more enjoyed for its contrast to the other" (pp. 151-152).

Fantastic reading, however, was still preferred, because Joy came through it; William Morris, Maeterlinck, and Yeats were favorites during these years, his late teens. Joy, however, was still something pagan, entirely remote from Christianity. Though to please his father, Lewis was confirmed and took his first communion, he was still a disbeliever. Beauty was one thing and Christianity was another—except in Wyvern Priory and Milton's verse, the two had never overlapped in all his experience. Indeed one seemed to suffocate the other (p. 172).

It was this antagonism which made Lewis' discovery of George Macdonald so important. In his autobiography he details the circumstances of this discovery, and he has also written of it in his preface to *George Macdonald: An Anthology.* It was a frosty October evening during his first term with Kirk. He was in the habit of walking over to Leatherhead and sometimes taking the train back, and as he stood on the railway platform in the cold twilight, he turned to the bookstall, to buy something for the weekend which lay ahead. There he found an Everyman edition of *Phantastes* by George Macdonald.

> A few hours later I knew that I had crossed a great frontier. I had already been waist deep in Romanticism; and likely enough, at any moment, to flounder in its darker and more evil forms, slithering down the steep descent that leads from the love of strangeness to that of eccentricity and thence to that of perversity. Now *Phantastes* was romantic enough in all conscience; but there was a difference. Nothing was at that time further from my thoughts than Christianity and I therefore had no notion what this difference really was. I was only aware that if this new world was strange, it was also homely and humble; that if this was a dream, it was a dream in which one at least felt strangely vigilant; that the whole book had about it a sort of cool, morning innocence, and also, quite unmistakably, a certain quality of Death, *good* Death.[13]

Lewis goes on to say that the quality which he found in Macdonald has turned out to be

> the quality of the real universe, the divine, magical, terrifying and ecstatic reality in which we all live. I should have been shocked in my 'teens if anyone had told me that what I learned to love in *Phantastes* was goodness. But now that I know, I see there was no deception. The deception is all the other way round—in that prosaic moralism which confines goodness to the

---

[13] *George Macdonald: An Anthology* (New York: Macmillan, 1948), pp. 20-21. A slightly abbreviated version of Lewis' preface is found in the Eerdmans edition of *Phantastes and Lilith*, Grand Rapids, 1964.

region of Law and Duty, which never lets us feel in our face the sweet air blowing from "the land of righteousness." (pp. 21-22)

This is a high tribute. And at first the reader may wonder if all this can possibly be found in Macdonald. As Lewis himself acknowledges, the Scottish novelist is often fumbling, verbose, and even florid. Yet a magical something is there and Lewis calls it Joy. This event of his teens took on added meaning in later years as is the wont of those events which later prove to have been crises. When one comes to see Lewis' indebtedness to Macdonald's thought, there can be no doubt that here he had crossed a frontier which would lead him to an unexpected place. As Gunnar Urang observes in his excellent *Shadows of Heaven, Phantastes* was for Lewis what the first sight of Beatrice had been for Dante. "Here begins the new life."

In the Infantry

During his second year with Kirk, Lewis took an examination at Oxford for a University College scholarship. He won it and entered in the summer of 1917. But before the term had passed he enlisted in the Infantry.

Most of the details relating to this two-year period we can pass over. They have little to do with Joy. Lewis was a second lieutenant and fought at the front until he was wounded. After spending some time in army hospitals, he was demobilized in December, 1918, soon after his twentieth birthday. Probably the most important thing that happened to him during this period, for our purposes at least, was again his reading. While hospitalized, he read with delight a book of G. K. Chesterton's essays. Here was humor which did not consist in inserted jokes or a general tone of forced heartiness but humor which was the "bloom on dialectic itself" (*Surprised by Joy*, p. 190). And though Lewis could not agree with what Chesterton said, he liked him, strangely enough, for his "goodness."

Another significant experience was that of reading Bergson in a convalescent camp on Salisbury Plain. Before that, Lewis says, the word "life" had had for him "pretty much the same connotations it had for Shelley in *The Triumph of Life*." He would not have understood "what Goethe meant by *des Lebens goldner Baum*." From Bergson he first learned to relish energy—"the resource, the triumphs, and even the insolence, of things that grow." He became more responsive to the art of "resonant, dogmatic, flaming, unanswerable people" like Beethoven, Titian, and Pindar. The "water-color world" of Morris and the "twilight" of Yeats' early poetry were not enough (*Surprised by Joy*, p. 198).

Student days at Oxford

In 1919 Lewis entered Oxford again, embarking upon "Greats" (the Honors School of Classics), and in that same year his first book, *Spirits in Bondage*, was published, under the pen name "Clive Hamilton." This was a collection of poems which were advertised at the time as the work of a soldier-poet, so it is possible that most of them were written while Lewis was in the army. These poems have attracted little attention, for they are written in a traditional idiom not popular in our day, and apparently Lewis had no wish to republish them. Some are obviously juvenilia, but many in the collection have merit and are particularly interesting in the light of his subsequent work.

Either implicit or frankly expressed in most of this verse is the Argument from Undesign and a bitter denunciation of the "red God" who will not pity nor lend an ear. No Swinburne or Hardy ever wrote more rebellious words.

> I cried out for the pain of man
> I cried out for my bitter wrath
> Against the hopeless life that ran
> Forever in a circling path.
> . . . .
> . . . I saw our planet, far and small
> Through endless depths of nothing fall
> A lonely pin-prick spark of light
> Upon the wide, enfolding night.[14]

[14] *Spirits in Bondage* (London: William Heinemann, 1919), "In Prison," p. 31.

Another in the same vein, "De Profundis," recalls the inspired blasphemy of *The Rubaiyat*: it is "but froth of folly" to rebel,

> For thou art Lord and hast the keys of Hell.
> Yet I will not bow down to thee nor love thee.
> For looking in my own heart I can prove thee.
> And know this frail, bruised thing is above thee.
> . . . .
> Laugh then and slay. Shatter all things of worth.
> Heap torment on torment for thy mirth
> Thou art not Lord while there are men on earth.
>
> (p. 34)

The poet praises the blessed escape from life's meaninglessness to be found in sleep ("To Sleep" and "Sonnet") or in "places of peace and discipline and dreaming" like Oxford, whose walls are built not out of "common stone"

> But out of all men's yearning and all prayer
> That She might live, eternally our own,
> The Spirit's stronghold—barred against despair.
>
> ("Oxford," pp. 82-83)

For to see and think with any sensitivity is to face suffering. Only the "solid people" escape, the good honest people who never feel "overwrought" before "man's mystery":

> Who water flowers and roll the lawn,
> And sit and sew and talk and smoke,
> And snore all through the summer dawn.
> . . . .
> Who sit of evenings by the fire
> . . . .
> And are not fretted by desire.
>
> ("In Praise of Solid People," pp. 62-65)

Herein lies the strange ambivalence of *Spirits in Bondage.* In most of the poems God is pictured as nonexistent or cruelly aloof from men. On the one hand, then, a denunciation of a God who does not exist, something close to nihilism. But on the other, a preoccupation with the meaning of desire, showing flashes of intuitive insight:

> . . . only the strange power
> Of unsought Beauty in some casual hour
> Can build a bridge of light or sound or form
> To lead you out of all this strife and storm.
> ("Dungeon Grates," pp. 40-41)

It is this "unsought Beauty" that holds out some promise of hope. Joy is the best comforter (though Lewis does not use this term as yet); one moment is enough:

> We know we are not made of mortal stuff.
> And we can bear all that comes after
>
> . . . .
> For we have seen the Glory—we have seen.
> ("Dungeon Grates," p. 42)

This moment of insight may come in dreams of the Western islands ("Hesperus," "Ode for New Year's Day") or in surrender to wonder and beauty in everyday circumstances. In "Song" as in "Dungeon Grates" there are suggestions that man's life has some transcendental significance, that the supernatural may live in the natural:

> Fairies must be in the woods
> Or the satyr's laughing broods—
> Tritons in the summer sea,
> Else how could the dead things be
> Half so lovely as they are?
> How could wealth of star on star
> Dusted o'er the frosty night
> Fill thy spirit with delight.
> (pp. 73-74)

This poem closes with very cryptic words indeed for one who has come so close to nihilism:

> Atoms dead could never thus
> Stir the human heart of us
> Unless the beauty that we see
> The veil of endless beauty be,
> Filled full of spirits that have trod
> Far hence along the heavenly sod
> And seen the bright footprints of God.
> (p. 74)

These last two poems may be among the last written just before the collection was published, for they lack the bitterness of tone so characteristic of most of the volume. It is possible that by the time these were written the foundations of Lewis' earlier atheism were beginning to crack. He says in *Surprised by Joy*: "A young man who wishes to remain a sound atheist cannot be too careful of his reading" (p. 191). And he confesses that by the time he returned to Oxford, Chesterton, Macdonald, and Bergson had begun to make the grim and defiant atheism of his teens look both less comprehensive and less honest than it once had.

A kind of popular realism ("If you kick a brick you know it's real") had so far existed side by side with a vivid awareness of Joy—one might say in logic-tight compartments. Now that he was studying philosophy, he began trying to reconcile the two, and under the influence of the New Psychology decided that all his "delectable mountains and western gardens" (*Surprised by Joy*, p. 203) were mere wish-fulfillment and nothing more. Dreams were futile and cursings just as futile; the best philosophy seemed to be a sort of Stoical Monism: we exist, the universe exists, we are in some sense one, and the deficiencies of the Whole can only be borne in quiet fortitude. For one cannot praise or blame the Whole; since he is part of it, his protests are only the voice of some Universal Thing futilely cursing itself. This "New Look," more sophisticated than the inconsistent nihilism of *Spirits in Bondage*, involved an attitude of acceptance which was comforting. But it depended largely on seeing Joy only as the perverse twinges of an overwrought nervous system, and though in theory Lewis accepted the Behavioristic explanation he continued to be haunted by *Sehnsucht*.

About this time some of his friends at Oxford became greatly interested in Rudolph Steiner's "Anthroposophy." Lewis was horrified, for Dr. Steiner's teaching involved divine beings, occult knowledge, and mystical exercises. One of the converts was tutor Owen Barfield, a very close and highly respected friend. His book *Poetic Diction* (1924) was to anticipate much of the semiotic aesthetic theory of Cassirer and Suzanne Langer,[15] and Lewis was later to dedicate *The Allegory of Love* to him as the "wisest and best" of his "unofficial teachers." To see Barfield get involved in such claptrap was too much—Lewis began a "war" with him which lasted over a period of years and which helped to clarify the thinking of both. This war, Lewis says, forever destroyed two elements in his thought: one, his "chronological snobbery," the uncritical acceptance of the intellectual climate of one's own age on the supposition that what is most recent is best; and two, his naive assumption that logical thought would lead to truth even if thought were only a subjective event having no objective ground of being.

One sees a reflection of Lewis' struggle with the intellectual climate of the twenties, particularly the Behavioristic explanation of rationality, in Book III of *The Pilgrim's Regress*. John meets a man named Sigismund, who is a son of Mr. Enlightenment but who has quarreled with his father. This young man flings John into a pit where all he can see is a stone giant the size of a mountain, the "Spirit of the Age." John discovers that the eyes of the giant have the property of rendering all things transparent. His fellow prisoners become skulls, larynxes, glands, blood vessels, and intestines. They, completely under the giant's control, speak of eggs as the menstruum of verminous fowl and of milk as being like sweat or dung. Whenever John protests they reply that argument is only an attempted rationalization of his desires. But they can argue eloquently, parroting each other's jargon, until John in despair is about to give up. Just then he is rescued by an armored rider wound in a cloak of blue, a rider whose name is Reason. Later on, in his theological works, Lewis was to make clear how it was that Reason kept him from the Behaviorism of the twenties. In *The Case for Christianity* he points out that if the validity of argument cannot be disproved without argument, one has not really set its usefulness aside, unless he believes that thought is merely a by-product of physio-

---

15 The close parallel is mentioned by Mrs. Langer in *Feeling and Form* (New York: Scribner's, 1953), p. 237.

chemical reactions. And if this is true, one man's physio-chemical reactions are as good as another's and it is silly to make any appeal to a common ground of rationality which can be trusted by both.

Lewis' recovery of some of his earlier respect for rea-son—which was paradoxically stimulated by Anthro-posophy's critique of Materialism—led him to seek a phi-losophy which would give a better account of reason. He began to find meaning in the Philosophic Idealism then dominant at Oxford. He came gradually to admit that "the whole universe was, in the last resort, mental" and that our logic was after all "participation in a cosmic logos" (*Surprised by Joy*, p. 209). The Absolute of T. H. Green, Bradley, and Bosanquet he could now believe in. Here was a way of transcending finitude, of reconciling contraries, for the Absolute was "there," whatever it might be.[16] (The last chapters of *Surprised by Joy* are harder going for some readers, for the intellectual bridge which at this point proved so helpful to Lewis—Hegelian or Idealistic philoso-phy—has all but vanished from the intellectual scene.)

In this mood he finished Greats in 1922 and took a fourth year, this time in the English School. Here he became a friend of Nevill Coghill, one of the most intelli-gent students he had ever known, who distressingly turned out to be a thoroughgoing supernaturalist Christian. Lewis' reading too seemed to conspire against his old suspicions of religion. Dr. Johnson, who seemed so utterly trust-worthy, turned out to have the same "kink" as Chesterton and Macdonald, and then there were Spenser, Milton, Sir Thomas Browne, Herbert, and Donne, who had it too. The most religious writers (Plato, Aeschylus, Virgil) were those in whom he found the most food, while those who did not "suffer from religion"—Shaw, Wells, Mill, Gibbon, Vol-taire—seemed thin gruel by comparison.

---

16 A crucial book in helping Lewis relate *Sehnsucht* to some form of Idealism was Samuel Alexander's *Space, Time, and Deity*. See the introduction to *C. S. Lewis: Images of His World* by Douglas Gilbert and Clyde S. Kilby (Grand Rapids: Eerdmans, 1973). Of all the materials on Lewis this pictorial book is the best introduction to Lewis the man.

> It wasn't that I didn't like them. They were all (especially Gibbon) entertaining; but hardly more. There seemed to be no depth in them. They were too simple. The roughness and density of life did not appear in their books. (*Surprised by Joy,* p. 214)

After receiving his B.A., with "firsts" in both classics and English, Lewis became a temporary lecturer in philosophy at University College. This was for one year (1924) while E. F. Carritt was in America.

In teaching philosophy Lewis began to discover that his watered-down Hegelianism simply did not serve. It was not that he sought a point of view to impose upon his students, but he knew he needed to clarify his own position if he were going to talk honestly and consistently about the views of others. He recalls a small happening about this time which made a profound impression upon him. One day, when Barfield and a pupil were having lunch with him in his room, Lewis happened to refer to philosophy as a "subject." "It wasn't a subject to Plato," said Barfield, "it was a way." The quick look of understanding from the pupil (now Dom Bede Griffiths) quickly revealed to Lewis his folly (p. 225). Intellectual and moral excellence should go together, but his present outlook made philosophy still an abstract thing which did not deal with "the roughness and density of life." Philosophic Idealism was hard to teach because as yet he had found no way to live it.

Fellow and tutor of Magdalen

In 1925 Lewis became fellow and tutor in English literature at Magdalen College. (He was later to receive his M.A. and become a special lecturer.) The following year he brought out his second book, *Dymer*, again under the name of Clive Hamilton. This was an allegorical fantasy in nine cantos of rhyme royal. The influence of Macdonald is evident and *Sehnsucht* is clearly the theme of the book.[17]

17 This is acknowledged in the preface Lewis wrote for the 1950 reprinting of the book, where he says that the particular form which his story took here depended on a peculiarity of his own history, his preoccupation from at least the age of six with "romantic longing—*Sehnsucht.*"

Dymer, a young man living in a Platonist republic where the gods have been "smothered down forever"[18] under the guidance of reason and science, has for nineteen years borne the chipping, moulding, and adorning of his soul by such a state. Then one April morning he bursts out laughing in the lecture-hall, strikes his teacher dead, and walks out of the city. Overwhelmed by the beauty of the countryside, he hears the music of longing and begins a pilgrimage in search of he knows not what. He proceeds to live through what Lewis called in his own experience "a dialectic of desire" in which each successive experience (human loves, art, occultism, etc.) proves Joy to be ever and ever more elusive. Particularly interesting is the section dealing with the house of the magician, in which one can see reflections of Lewis' war with Barfield. In the ninth canto Dymer is killed by a wild beast which has been pursuing him for some time. At sunrise the springing of flowers from his grave and the singing of birds signal some victory—a sort of resurrection or taking on of immortality—though the meaning is not clear. This is probably because at this point in Lewis' thought resurrection could be little more than an artistic device, artificially introduced.

During the late twenties Lewis' friendships with fellow tutors Hugo Dyson and J. R. R. Tolkien, who were both Roman Catholics, continued to break down his prejudices against Christianity. He read Chesterton's *The Everlasting Man* and Rudolf Otto's *The Idea of the Holy*—two books whose influence on him seemed to increase with time. And early in 1926, when Philosophical Idealism seemed to be wearing rather thin, he heard a convinced atheist make a statement which was, like the books, to gather weight as time went on. This man, sitting beside the fire in Lewis' rooms at Magdalen, remarked that the evidence for the historicity of the Gospels was actually surprisingly good. " 'Rum thing,' he went on. 'All that stuff of Frazer's about the Dying God. Rum thing. It almost looks as if it had really happened once' " (*Surprised by Joy*, pp. 223-224). This idea gave Lewis a "jolt" which he was unable to

---

[18] *Dymer* (London: J. M. Dent, 1926), p. 2.

dismiss. Was it possible that the Absolute was actually the Christian God, that in Him the best of all the myths of paganism and of Christianity were fulfilled? Philosophic Idealism could be talked, even felt, but it seemed impossible to live it. Even with such pantheistic overtones as Lewis' beliefs had recently taken on, particularly in his work with the Romantic poets, Idealism was undeniably too fuzzy and abstract to touch life at all the points where he had discovered meaning and significance. Indeed he was finding it to be a "quasi-religion" which was "all a one-way street; all *eros* steaming up, but no *agape* darting down" (p. 210). Intellectually, he knew that there had to be a focusing—and though the full weight of the long tradition of theism seemed to be bearing down upon him emotionally, he was afraid of admitting any transcendental interferer—he only wanted to be left alone.

> You must picture me alone in that room in Magdalen, night after night, feeling, whenever my mind lifted even for a second from my work, the steady, unrelenting approach of Him whom I so earnestly desired not to meet. That which I greatly feared had at last come upon me. In the Trinity Term of 1929 I gave in, and admitted that God was God, and knelt and prayed: perhaps, that night, the most dejected and reluctant convert in all England. (pp. 228-229)

This conversion experience, Lewis says, was primarily to Theism, not to Christianity in any full sense. Although he began attending the services of the Anglican parish church and his college chapel, it was not with pleasure, for he was both anti-ecclesiastical and constitutionally inept at anything "churchy." But he went because he was convinced that as a theist he ought to fly some kind of flag. One day, about two years later, he and his brother were motorcycling to Whipsnade Zoo. When he set out he did not believe that Jesus Christ was the Son of God and when he got there he did.[19] To retrace the questioning and study which went into this final step is impossible here. He has discussed these matters in several of his theological studies.

---

[19] *C. S. Lewis: Images of His World*, p. 12.

And Lewis makes clear in the autobiography and elsewhere that faith was ultimately something given to him. It was reasoning which led him on and on, but in the last resort, the initiative did not seem to be all in his control. He says, however, that he recalls moments when there was a decisiveness in the air, when he knew he was directing his will toward or against something.

He also makes it clear that at his conversion he had no assurance that Joy was something intimately connected with Christianity. Indeed he was not sure, in 1929 that Joy had anything to do with religious experience at all. He only knew the search had led him irrevocably to where he now was and Joy in itself now seemed less important. But he was gradually—with far less of the self-consciousness which had dominated his search—to discover its connection with all that seemed most authentic in his experience.

III THE BAPTIZED IMAGINATION: Lewis' Later Work

> What we learn from experience depends upon the kind of philosophy we bring to experience. It is therefore useless to appeal to experience before we have settled, as well as we can, the philosophical question.
>
> —C. S. Lewis, *Miracles*

The name of C. S. Lewis was little known outside Oxford until the late 1930's. His early poems and the allegorical *Pilgrim's Regress* had only a slim audience, and it was not until the publication of *The Allegory of Love* in 1936 that his real stature was recognized. Within the next few years he published two other books of literary criticism [1] and a "space and time story" (Lewis' term) with theological overtones, *Out of the Silent Planet.*

In 1940 appeared his study of the philosophical problem which had haunted his boyhood, *The Problem of Pain.* And a year later his *Screwtape Letters* (which defy classification) began to be published serially in *The Guardian.* This was during the blitz, when Londoners made their way each night to bomb shelters with the knowledge that by morning Britain might be no more. The BBC, impressed by the strong logic of Lewis' study of the Argument from Undesign and by the urbane wit of the satirical *Letters,*

---

[1] *The Personal Heresy* and *Rehabilitations,* a collection of essays most of which defend some author or movement recently under attack.

asked him to deliver a series of radio talks on theology. In the early forties Lewis gave a total of twenty-nine such talks which were later published.[2]

During World War II Lewis also lectured on theology at RAF bases, an assignment not much to his liking. He accepted these "missioning" assignments, both on radio and at military camps, with great hesitation—first because he had been outside the Christian fold for many years and also because he did not consider himself properly qualified for such work. But the precariousness of life itself during the war years made him feel that he had to do it. He has since referred to his launching out into popular theology as an example of "the unscrupulousness of God."[3] That he had indeed become a leading lay theologian was recognized in 1946 when St. Andrew's University in Scotland awarded him the honorary degree of Doctor of Divinity.

The Inklings

One cannot understand Lewis' theology or literary development without knowing of a small circle of close friends who met weekly in an Oxford pub from 1939 to the 1960's. This group began meeting when the Oxford University Press was evacuated from London to Oxford because of the blitz. With the press came Charles Williams, one of its editors, who was also a poet, critic, and novelist. He seems to have been one of those rare individuals who have both strong convictions and the charm to present them without arrogance or defensiveness. He was not only a genius and a likable companion but also, judging from the word of many who knew him, a genuine saint. Until his death in 1945, he had a profound influence not only on Lewis but on all who were members of this circle or closely connected with it—in particular, Fr. Gervase Mathew, J. R. R. Tolkien, Owen Barfield, and Hugo Dyson. The

[2] These talks were published in the United States under the titles *The Case for Christianity*, *Christian Behavior*, and *Beyond Personality*, later to be combined under one title, *Mere Christianity*, for which Lewis wrote a special introduction in 1952.

[3] "Don vs. Devil," *Time*, 50 (Sept. 8, 1947), 72.

Inklings, as they have sometimes been called,[4] gathered for cider and good talk from eleven to one every Tuesday morning. And sometimes the conversations were taken up again in the evenings in rooms at Exeter or Magdalen. The group was a fluctuating one, usually numbering around a half dozen, sometimes including students as well as dons.[5]

This circle was bound together particularly by a common interest in writing and in the nature of language and myth. And they sought together an understanding of Christian theology which would be more relevant to aesthetics than Christian theology had often been. Dorothy Sayers, while not a member of this group, was, through her admiration of Williams' work in particular, closely connected with it, and the Inklings were deeply influenced by her religious works, especially by her endeavors toward a Christian aesthetic. Under the stimulation of these shared concerns, Williams wrote his *All Hallows Eve,* Tolkien his *Lord of the Rings,* and Lewis *The Great Divorce,* the Narnia books, and his interplanetary trilogy. The second book of this trilogy, *Perelandra,* was read to Tolkien and Williams for criticism as he wrote it. In fact, all of Lewis' fiction shows the influence of these two writers, and the most prolific period of his career was during the early forties, when Williams especially seemed to act as a catalyst for Lewis' writing.

In *Essays Presented to Charles Williams* Lewis tells how the friendship with Williams began in an exchange of letters, Lewis expressing his enthusiasm for Williams' early novel, *The Place of the Lion,* and the other writing of his appreciation for *The Allegory of Love.* When Williams came to Oxford, it was natural that they should become close friends. Lewis says he discovered in this man a "principle of liveliness and cohesion . . . an 'esemplastic' force" (in Coleridgean language) which could bind a group of friends together and stimulate them to tasks they had little dreamed of.[6]

---

4 Lewis dedicated *The Problem of Pain* to "the Inklings."

5 Chad Walsh, *C. S. Lewis: Apostle to the Skeptics,* pp. 15-16.

6 *Essays Presented to Charles Williams,* edited by C. S. Lewis (Grand Rapids: Eerdmans, 1966), p. xi.

Charles Williams' "Romantic Theology"

Atheism had appealed to Lewis as a dogmatic system, something one could prove by hardhitting dialectic. His earliest efforts in theology after he became a practicing Anglican show that he would have liked to make Christianity as neat and foolproof as atheism had once seemed. In *The Pilgrim's Regress* and some of the radio talks there is a tendency toward a brittle dogmatism which knows its own logical respectability.[7] As Lewis came under the influence of Williams' eclectic thought with its strongly mystical bent, certain important changes resulted—changes which might well have occurred apart from Williams, though the process would likely have taken longer. In the day-to-day contacts with this friend who lived his loyalties contagiously yet without seeking to defend them with compulsive logic, Lewis' ideas were reshaped in several ways.

First, theology became less and less something which could be completely "domesticated" by reason. In Williams' thought there was room for paradoxes, ironies, and tensions which the early Lewis had little glimpsed. Williams, for example, in discussing the Book of Job with Lewis once compared Job's comforters to "the sort of people who write books on the Problem of Pain."[8] He was uneasy about logical, systematized expositions of soul-troubling mysteries. His theology found expression mostly in fiction and poetry.

Second, Williams' tastes were capable of encompassing great variety. As Lewis himself has pointed out:

> He excelled at showing you the little grain of truth or felicity in some passage generally quoted for ridicule while at the same time he fully enjoyed the absurdity or, contrariwise, at detecting the little falsity or dash of silliness in a passage which you, and he also, admired. He was both a debunker and (if I may coin the word) a "rebunker."[9]

---

[7] An early critique of Lewis' theology gives examples of this tendency in the broadcast talks. See E. L. Allen's "The Theology of C. S. Lewis," *Modern Churchman*, 34 (Jan.-March, 1945), 318f.

[8] Lewis' preface to *Essays Presented to Charles Williams*, p. xiii.

[9] *Ibid.*, p. xi.

It is interesting that Lewis apologizes in the second edition of *The Regress* for the bitterness of some of the passages in that book. This bitterness is understandable in that it is reserved for those things he had once embraced and then left behind as heresies. But it is possible that Lewis would never have seen the uncharitableness of some of his attacks had it not been for his association with Williams. Williams was able to find some good in several of the things Lewis had derided. The skeptic, the mystic, and the Counter-Romantic were treated with greater understanding and sympathy by Williams and eventually by Lewis.

And third, Williams' outlook definitely increased Lewis' interest in *Sehnsucht* and aided Lewis in developing this rather substantial mystical complement to his tough-minded theology. Williams considered himself a "romantic theologian," by which he meant one who tries to be theological about romance. And Lewis had for many years been interested in the theological implications of Romanticism. It was therefore inevitable that there should be many fruitful conversations on this subject. Lewis sees his friend's attitude here as thoroughly ambivalent; Williams, he says, could be grouped with the Counter-Romantics in that he saw an "untheologicalized romanticism (like Plato's 'unexamined life') to be sterile and mythological." Yet he strongly rejected the modern attitude toward the Romantics, for he believed the Romanticism which they were "rejecting as senile to be really immature, and looked for a coming of age where they were huddling up a hasty and not very generous funeral."[10]

As a writer matures he often tends to qualify his earlier positions; the balder ideas of youth give way to subtleties and a richer suggestiveness. I see this in Lewis, especially under Williams' influence. After Williams' death in 1945 there was a falling off in Lewis' productivity and possibly in his powers. Theologians have found his *Miracles* (1947) a rather disappointing book,[11] and it is interesting that

10 *Essays Presented to Charles Williams*, p. vi.
11 W. Norman Pittenger makes this observation in his "Critique of C. S.

between the year of Williams' death and the publication in 1958 of Lewis' book on the Psalter there is little which was not at least begun while Williams was alive. The Narnia books for children, though published in the fifties, were written in the forties; a good deal of *Surprised by Joy* was also written in the forties. Lewis was of course busy for many years on his history of English literature in the sixteenth century. This may be the main reason for the apparent gap. But it seems pertinent that it was not until the later 1950's that Lewis came back to sustained exposition in theology or to fiction. It also seems that time has vindicated Williams even at points where he and Lewis would once have disagreed. *Reflections on the Psalms* is a more temperate and charitable book than *The Regress* and it is far less "pat" than parts of the radio talks. And *Till We Have Faces* has a quality of mystery, a subtlety and richness not to be found in the earlier novels, haunting as they are.

The impact of Owen Barfield

The other key influence among Lewis' friends was Owen Barfield, his solicitor and friendly intellectual combatant for more than forty years. R. J. Reilly in his fine study *Romantic Religion* shows Barfield as the Coleridge-like theorizer for the Inklings.[12] He was the one who got them thinking most deeply about the imagination, the relations of imagination, reason, and language, and who got across not a little of the Anthroposophy he had adapted from Rudolph Steiner.

With Reilly's help I find several principles in Lewis' thought which seem to have developed through Barfield's influence:

1. The reality of thought as beyond the neurological, as having connections with extrinsic reality. Barfield develops

---

Lewis," *The Christian Century,* 75 (Oct. 1, 1958), 1104-1107. That theologians have been disappointed in *Miracles* may be because they expect it to go further than it does; it is subtitled "A Preliminary Study."

[12] Athens: University of Georgia, 1971, especially ch. 2.

Steiner's idea that the mind is related to thought as the eye is to light. No one suggests that light is simply something that goes on in the eye. Light is really there and thought is real also. For if something like Plato's World of Ideas or Jung's Race Memory does not exist, then thinking may be only the twitching of brain tissue. Lewis hammers this point home repeatedly in his books, especially in *Mere Christianity* and *The Abolition of Man* but also in *That Hideous Strength* and numerous essays.

2. The counterattack on chronological snobbery. Barfield believed that mind or spirit preceded matter, that modern man is impoverished by his lack of mythic and metaphoric consciousness, that presentism is a sure way to sharply limit one's understanding of reality. Lewis elaborates this idea further in, for example, his introduction to a translation of St. Athanasius.

3. The fact that spiritual life is immanent in phenomena. Barfield explains how the European mind has cut itself loose from its environment and has become less and less the actor, more often the spectator. Now this is an idea Lewis frequently voiced in his early poetry, but it seems certain that Barfield's corroboration of it gave him the courage to embrace it in prose, where one is philosophically more vulnerable. For Lewis' best discussion of the subject see his preface to D. E. Harding's *The Hierarchy of Heaven and Earth: A New Diagram of Man in the Universe* (New York: Harper, 1952).

4. The necessity of knowing through the imagination. Barfield develops this idea in a way which could have come from Coleridge, and though it was uphill work to defend it when Barfield wrote *Poetic Diction* in 1928, the idea seems to have many supporters today among scientists, especially physicists. Lewis mentions in *Surprised by Joy* and elsewhere what an important book *Poetic Diction* was for him, and Barfield may well have dedicated it to him precisely because these two anti-selves had thrashed out so many of its ideas so vehemently.

Of course, Barfield also has some key ideas which Lewis did not accept: the way Goethe used the esemplastic imagination, the notion that God Himself undergoes an evolution of consciousness (Lewis' uneasiness about Teilhard de Chardin suggests he could not follow Barfield closely on that concept), and the idea that the Word is the cosmic process on its way from original (unconscious) to final (conscious) participation in God (though it is possible to find this idea in *Till We Have Faces*).

As dazzling as some of Barfield's ideas are, they appear to be Platonism again (or common sense, some would say), philologically considered in terms which make sense in our day. Lewis' Platonism is unmistakable and it is not surprising that he would find reading Kierkegaard "like walking in sawdust." Lewis found in Platonism a comprehensive way to reconcile reason's dialectic with the reasons of the heart. To settle for anything less than such a reconciliation, he felt, would be to betray his experience of art, mind, and the everyday world.

The influence of older literary works on Lewis' theology

It would be a mistake, however, to see Williams and Barfield as the only important influences on Lewis. The most important long-term influence on Lewis' thought was the work of George Macdonald. In the preface to his anthology of Macdonald's work Lewis says: "I have never concealed the fact that I regard him as my master: indeed I fancy I have never written a book in which I did not quote from him."[13]

Macdonald, who because of his many novels of Scottish life has usually been relegated to the "Kailyard School," is actually a far more complex figure than that classification suggests. As a mythmaker and theologian he was destined to be appreciated more in our time than in his own. His mythopoeic narratives such as *Phantastes* and *Lilith* and some of his poetry and sermons fairly vibrate with a spiritual exaltation and unselfconscious goodness quite rare in literature. Though his work is often faulty as art, yet his great warmth and integrity somehow transcend

---

13 In *The Great Divorce* (New York: Macmillan, 1946) it is George Macdonald who acts as spokesman for the Solid People (the redeemed company of Heaven).

these faults—at least for those who seek to understand the religious function of the imagination.

It is precisely here that Macdonald was stimulating and helpful to Lewis. The theology of this defrocked Scots Presbyterian in some respects anticipated what Liberal Protestantism was to become. His theology is often amorphous. Yet Lewis admires him still—for his ethical insights, the deeply devotional bent of his thought, and his ability to make the crimson and gold of mythopoeic never-never lands the vehicle of Christian truth.

In addition to Macdonald's contribution, it must be pointed out that Lewis, though having no formal training in theology, brings to any discussion of Christian doctrine a great deal that he has learned in Medieval and Renaissance literature. Long before he became a Christian he had read deeply in Dante, Spenser, Milton, and George Herbert. And he had been tremendously excited by these writers in spite of their obvious Christianity. In *Spirits in Bondage* the young Lewis wrote that on the reader of Milton

> Falls the weird spirit of unexplained delight,
> New mystery in every shady place,
> In every whispering tree a nameless grace,
> New rapture on the windy seaward height.[14]

His enthusiasm for Milton continued in spite of critical attacks on that writer, and it was out of this enthusiasm that he wrote his well-known *Preface to Paradise Lost* in 1942.

When Lewis began to be interested in Christianity, he studied St. Augustine, Hooker, Thomas Traherne, William Law's *Serious Call, The Imitation,* and Tacitus' *Theologica Germanica.* His thinking for the most part was shaped by older writers whose ideas have lived on in works well known to students of literature. This meant both an advantage and a disadvantage in Lewis' ability to understand and communicate Christian doctrine. His theological works aim at the simplicity and clearness of Augustine or Hooker,

14 "Milton Read Again," *Spirits in Bondage,* pp. 50-51.

untrammeled by the deliberate ambiguities of some contemporary theologians. Yet because Lewis' roots were primarily in these older periods, he had less to say to those caught up in the Existentialist theology of his time.

While he agreed at many points with men like Kierkegaard, Maritain, and Berdyaev, he found them repetitive and muddy compared with earlier theologians. He did, however, admire Buber and Marcel (again with some reservation about repetition) and was deeply influenced by Otto's *The Idea of the Holy*, and to a lesser extent by Nygren's *Agape and Eros*.[15] Existentialism in general did not appeal to Lewis because he believed that this recurring emphasis in philosophy, if carried to its logical end (e.g., Kierkegaard's reworking of "I believe because it is absurd"), imperils reason—and for the Christian, needlessly so. To be sure, Lewis does not believe that reason, unaided by God's grace, can lead man automatically to the truth. No such autonomy can be his when the ultimate initiative lies always in God's hands.[16] But though "men by wisdom knew not God" (to quote St. Paul), Lewis insists that truth as it is given by God cannot be understood apart from reason. In fact, the good Existentialist cannot analyze his dilemma or argue against the primacy of reason without using reason.

It is significant, I believe, that Lewis never embraced the Liberal Protestantism of the late nineteenth and early twentieth century. Because he did not, he did not find it necessary to react violently against rationalism in order to rediscover his faith. It was doubtless this reaction which gave so much impetus to Christian Existentialism or Neo-Orthodoxy, as it is sometimes called, and which made Kierkegaard's overstated corrective so meaningful to this theological generation.[17]

[15] Lewis relates this information in a letter (dated Oct. 13, 1958) which he wrote in response to my queries in this connection.

[16] This view is implicit in all of Lewis' theological works and is explicitly set forth in *Beyond Personality* (New York: Macmillan, 1945), p. 12, and in *Surprised by Joy*, especially the last five chapters.

[17] See Walsh's discussion of Lewis on this point, pp. 108-114.

Lewis' basic theological orientation

Lewis' insistence on reason has led some to regard him as essentially Thomist in his theology. And Lewis does not deny the profound influence of the *Summa* on his thought. He says that he used it for years as a sort of dictionary of medieval belief.[18] But with a Thomist idea as with a Platonic one, he believes that one should argue *to* it rather than *from* it.[19] He does not see Christianity as dependent upon any philosophical system, though various systems have certainly lent themselves to interpreting the faith. The *Summa* did this for the Middle Ages, and the Hegelian dialectic helped to frame and answer theological questions for some nineteenth-century Christians.

Another aspect of Lewis' thought which has led some critics to regard him as essentially Thomist is his untiring attack on "chronological snobbery"—something which he came to under Barfield's influence, and which has been misinterpreted as "medievalism." Lewis is of course very much at home in the Middle Ages, by training and special interests. But what he has said against contemporary trends is not based on a Utopian view of that period but rather on his strong reaction against the uncritical acceptance of the contemporary climate of opinion.[20] He continually seeks to remind the reader how little space in time is the last fifty years or so and he believes that there is no better way to avoid provincialism than by reading the old books—at least two for every contemporary work.[21]

In answer to those who have read his books as modern restatements of Aquinas, Lewis says that the appearance of a strong Thomist influence is really due to the fact that he

18 Letter to author dated Oct. 13, 1958.

19 Lewis takes this stand in his comments on Plato in *The Personal Heresy*, pp. 51-52.

20 In his inaugural address at Cambridge he said: "I think no class of men are less enslaved to the past than historians. The unhistorical are usually, without knowing it, enslaved to a fairly recent past." See *De Descriptione Temporum* (Cambridge: Cambridge, 1955), p. 19.

21 See Lewis' preface to a new translation of Athanasius' *The Incarnation of the Word of God* (New York: Macmillan, 1946).

has often (especially on ethics) followed Aristotle where Aquinas also followed Aristotle. "Aquinas," he says, "and I were, in fact, at the same school—I don't say in the same class! And I had read the *Ethics* long before I ever worked at the *Summa*."[22]

My own reading of Lewis shows him to be Thomist,[23] Aristotelian, Platonist, or Neo-Kantian (though rarely the latter) only as something in each of these approaches serves him as a tool of thought. I suspect that on the whole his tough-minded theology finds its logical sanctions in Aristotelian analysis.[24] But one cannot say this without immediately balancing the statement with the observation that many aspects of Lewis' thought are Platonic to the core. To say this is, I believe, not to suggest any shifting partisanship on his part but rather to acknowledge the complexity of truth and the necessity of stating it not always in terms of "either . . . or" but sometimes in terms of "both . . . and."

This very point is well illustrated by the variety of influences which helped to shape Lewis' thought after his conversion to Christianity. Macdonald and Williams were most important, but Aquinas, Augustine, Traherne, and Coventry Patmore were influential too. And Lewis says that he learned also from I. A. Richards, Jung, Edwyn Bevan,[25] and a great diversity of other writers. He would agree with George Macdonald, who said, "Truth is truth,

22 Letter to author dated Oct. 13, 1958.

23 Charles Hartshorne has noted Lewis' dissatisfaction with the Thomist doctrine of the impassivity of God, although he feels that Lewis moved toward a Thomist metaphysics by unjustly confusing pantheism with panentheism. See "Philosophy and Orthodoxy," *Ethics*, 54 (July, 1944), 295-298.

24 Lewis is, however, sharply critical of Aristotle in *The Allegory of Love*: "Aristotle is, before all, the philosopher of divisions. His effect on his greatest disciple [Aquinas], as M. Gilson has traced it, was to dig new chasms between God and the world, between human knowledge and reality, between faith and reason. Heaven began, under this dispensation, to seem farther off. The danger of Pantheism grew less: the danger of mechanical Deism came a step nearer. It is almost as if the first, faint shadow of Descartes, or even of 'our present discontents' had fallen across the scene" (London: Oxford, 1938), p. 88.

25 He commends Bevan's *Symbolism and Belief* and Owen Barfield's *Poetic Diction* as basic studies in his *Miracles: A Preliminary Study* (New York: Macmillan, 1947), p. 86.

whether from the lips of Jesus or Balaam."[26] Thus pigeon-holing or blacklisting any writer is beside the point if one believes in the capacity of reason to discover truth under divine guidance.

Yet Lewis also acknowledges the necessity of balancing and guiding one's rational conclusions by such intuitive insights as are given.[27] In an essay on the nature of metaphorical language, he once summarized his position thus:

> I am a rationalist. For me reason is the natural organ of truth; but imagination is the organ of meaning. Imagination, producing new metaphors or revivifying old, is not the cause of truth, but its condition.[28]

In other words, although one cannot discuss anything intelligently without the use of reason, the metaphorical condition of language, particularly theological language, necessitates that the highest truths be expressed in symbols which are not rationally but imaginatively understood. It is here that Lewis is indebted to the Platonic tradition with its teaching that it is not until concepts have been turned into images that the real appears to the human mind. In the same essay Lewis observes that Kant and Spinoza may not be so literal, accurate, and unmystical as they think. "Plato, one of the great masters of metaphor, may have a higher percentage of meaning."[29]

Meaning then for Lewis comes through both reason and imagination. And it is this dual approach which makes him unusual in an age when it has been fashionable either to damn reason and live for art or to reject artistic statement as empirically meaningless.

26 *George Macdonald: An Anthology*, p. 27.

27 See *Miracles*, p. 108.

28 "Bluspels and Flalansferes," *Rehabilitations* (London: Oxford, 1939), p. 158.

29 "Bluspels and Flalansferes," *Rehabilitations*, p. 167.

Lewis' approach to Biblical images

I was startled recently to hear a well-published philosopher of science say that he had reluctantly come to see that literature and not science was the best way to approach philosophy, that he had begun to read avidly in Eliot, Dante, and Milton—to discover that they were "doing philosophy" in the profoundest sense.

Today's philosophical language fails to reach either the concrete or the metaphysical, which are accessible nonetheless through literature. Lewis evidently believed with Owen Barfield that there is a psychophysical parallelism in the universe. Primitive man did not differentiate himself as Subject from the world as Object. Nor did he divide the phenomenal (sensible) world from the noumenal (invisible) world. He did not have to split *how* he experienced the objective world from *what* he experienced or *how he experienced.* He was able to experience and express through metaphors, which were vivid and full of the discovery of psychophysical connections.

Because today's philosophical language tries to prune away the metaphorical, it impoverishes itself in a way which would be unthinkable in Biblical language. Lewis is especially instructive on the subject of Biblical inspiration and makes room in his approach for the sort of archetypal experiencing to which *Sehnsucht* belongs. He took seriously the progressive nature of God's gradual self-revelation. He did not consider truth or value to be tied necessarily to historical or scientific accuracy, though the value of something like the Incarnation would of course be bound up in historical actuality. But it is through the *purport* of the images that revelation comes.

Because of the literary character of the Bible, some kinds of demythologizing are important. Yet images must be preserved for there to be revelation. And if one cannot hold onto the idea without thinking "literally," i.e., in terms of the images, Lewis says to go ahead and be literal. In the end such an approach can address the whole person in a way that theological abstraction cannot. Lewis adds that correct thinking can even be accompanied by false imaginings (see *Miracles*, ch. 10, "Horrid Red Things"). Lewis confessed he often pictured London as being Euston Station—a false picture, yes, but somehow it carried the purport of London for him and he was not at all unclear as to what the city of London was like.[30]

Lewis' own highly imagistic style addresses the whole person. When Lewis pursues a puzzling theological doctrine in his sermons, he achieves some of the best non-fiction prose of the century, worthy of the tradition of Donne and Launcelot Andrewes. As Roger Lancelyn Green observes, only Lewis and Archbishop William Temple could fill the Oxford University Church to capacity—and rhetorical brilliance was no small part of the explanation.

Lewis' later years

When Lewis accepted the chair of Medieval and Renaissance Literature at Cambridge in 1955, he said in his inaugural address that he would seek to fill the post as one of the surviving "Old Western men." He saw himself as belonging to a vanishing species—the traditional sort of scholar, trained in classical learning, specialist in some period "remote" from our own yet student of many disciplines, and defender of the humane values against the encroachment of technology, intellectual relativism gone rampant, and a general disrespect for the past. He observes that we have lived to see the second death of classical learning and predicts no future renaissance. This sober analysis of the trend of our age did not, however, deter Lewis in his work as one of the last of the Old Western men. His monumental *English Literature in the Sixteenth Century* was published in 1954 and continues to create a stir among Renaissance scholars because of the many tacit assumptions which it challenges.

The publication of that book had one happy side-benefit. The lady who helped Lewis with the proofs be-

---

30 For a more detailed discussion of Lewis' approach to the Bible see William Luther White's *The Image of Man in C. S. Lewis* (Nashville: Abingdon, 1969) and Larry Cunningham's *C. S. Lewis: Defender of the Faith* (Philadelphia: Westminster, 1967).

came his wife in 1956. He had known Joy Davidman Gresham for several years, first as a visitor from America who, having been very active with her former husband in the Communist Party, had then forsaken Communism and become a Christian—partly through reading his books—and then as a student at Oxford. Miss Davidman, herself a writer, was drawn to Lewis' books particularly because of his interest in *Sehnsucht*. For she too from her teens had had glimpses of a land which exists beyond some unfound door. As a girl it was fairyland, as a student it was art, as a young writer it was the Comes-the-Revolution Country, and then when each of these had failed to fulfill the dream, she discovered in Lewis' *Pilgrim's Regress* what the dialectic of desire signifies for the Christian. The story of her intellectual pilgrimage is a fascinating one; she has told it in an essay called "The Longest Way Round."[31]

It seems highly probable that Miss Davidman encouraged Lewis' curiosity about *Sehnsucht*, for practically all of his later work gave attention to it. It is the main thread of *Surprised by Joy* and is important in various essays as well as in *Till We Have Faces*. Also, many of the twenty poems which appeared in *Punch* between 1946 and 1954 (under the pseudonym "N. W.") are preoccupied with the *Sehnsucht* theme.

In some ways the last eight years of Lewis' life (after he had left the Oxford faculty) were his happiest. Not only his marriage but his acceptance among Cambridge colleagues seemed to diminish the slightly hectoring tone of some of his earlier work. At Oxford his activities as a Christian layman had made him suspect—to be a lay theologian writing popular books was simply not done by Oxonians. Helen Gardner remarks the change at Cambridge in her British Academy monograph and praises Lewis for encompassing "a dozen cities of the mind."

But these dozen cities were fastened to a "dying animal," and on November 22, 1963, Lewis endured his "going hence." It was the same day that John F. Kennedy

---

31 This essay appeared in *These Found the Way*, edited by David W. Soper (Philadelphia: Westminster, 1951).

and Aldous Huxley also died. In Lewis' funeral service the following verse from Psalm 84 was read: "My soul hath a desire and longing to enter into the courts of the Lord." The longing which he had felt as a boy and which had made a golden skein all through the experiences of his life had now brought him at last to the City of the King, where in the words of Psalm 84 his whole being cried out "with joy to the living God."

It is difficult to predict what literary venture Lewis might have turned to next. He had tried almost all the usual genres and worked many veins of thought. One thing, however, seems certain: his tough-minded theology had been greatly deepened and qualified by his preoccupation with the aspect of mystical tradition which is the subject of this study. It is striking that in Lewis the two seem so compatible. Why this is so and how this "dialectic of desire" finds expression in his imaginative works it will be my task to explore in the next three chapters.

IV OPULENT MELANCHOLY AND THE QUEST

I am never merry when I hear sweet music.
—Jessica in *The Merchant of Venice*

When Goethe wrote of "blissful longing" and Thomas Wolfe of "the full delight of loneliness," they were not engaged simply in a perverse juggling of words. E. M. W. Tillyard says there is in human experience a "primal Joy-Melancholy" which is not to be confused with mere escape feeling.[1] And though this "primal Joy-Melancholy" cannot be presented in any symbolism bound to the logic of discourse, it is still a familiar content in poetry (Keats' "Ode on Melancholy" is a classic statement). The inadequacy of literal description to deal with this emotion, or complex of emotions, has led some logical analysts to question its existence. But as Suzanne Langer points out, literal description by its very nature emphasizes the separateness of Joy and Melancholy, while artistic forms can be ambivalent in that "emotional opposites—joy and grief, desire and fear, and so forth—are often very similar in their dynamic structure, and reminiscent of each other."[2]

As I noted in Chapter II, Lewis reveals his awareness of this ambivalent attitude in his earliest published work,

---

[1] E. M. W. Tillyard, *Poetry Direct and Oblique* (London: Chatto and Windus, 1934, revised 1945), p. 51.

[2] Suzanne Langer, *Feeling and Form*, p. 242.

Spirits in Bondage (1919), and elaborates on the attitude in *Dymer* (1926). By the time he wrote *The Pilgrim's Regress* (1933), the *Sehnsucht* motif had become a well-worked-out theory having definite philosophical implications. But although his exploration of the attitude antedates Tillyard's discussion, it was not until Lewis did an essay on William Morris in the late thirties that he applied his thinking on *Sehnsucht* to practical criticism.

Lewis had been an enthusiastic admirer of Morris from boyhood. Several of the poems in *Spirits in Bondage,* notably "Ballade Mystique" and "Noon," show his influence. And the same Germanic "hard-bitten-ness," sober understatement, and cool watercolor effects are to be found in *The Pilgrim's Regress.* Ironically Morris, in so many ways the complete pagan, had early communicated to Lewis the sense of "Joy" which was to lead him to Christianity. In the essay on Morris in *Rehabilitations* he tries to account for the continuing attraction he discovered in that poet's work and refers for the first time to "Northernness," that exultant yet strangely tragic emotion which he associates with Tegner's *Drapa,* Norse mythology, and Wagner's operas. He says that for Morris it is not unhappiness but happiness which is the cause of misgiving, for it makes us "once more mindful that the sweet days die." [3] Morris to be sure presents no theories about *Sehnsucht.* He is preeminently, Lewis says, a writer whose work "is the fresh fruit of naive experience, uncontaminated by theorizing" (*Rehabilitations,* p. 53). In Morris there are no conclusions except that "we must labor for the kindred and love the earth and the world with all our souls." This love of the world will tempt desire to sail beyond its frontiers, and "those who sail must look back from shoreless seas to find that they have abandoned their sole happiness. Those who return must find that happiness once more embittered by its mortality, must long again" (pp. 51-52).

---

[3] "William Morris," *Rehabilitations and Other Essays,* p. 46. I speak of this essay as Lewis' first use of *Sehnsucht* in his critical writing. Actually he refers to it in *The Allegory of Love* (in a discussion of the *Romance of the Rose,* pp. 75-76), but the reference is brief and does not distinguish *Sehnsucht* from the larger Romantic attitude.

This "hithering and withering," as Lewis calls it, goes on inevitably; yet, he says, Morris does not reject the world—his glimpses of Desire are "too irregular and shot full of colours to be compared to the sad Buddhist wheel"(p. 52). Lewis therefore concludes that although Morris has no great capacity for analysis, it is hard to "get behind" his vision of the world:

> No full-grown mind wants optimism or pessimism—philosophies of the nursery when they are not philosophies of the clinic; but to have presented in one vision the ravishing sweetness and the heart-breaking melancholy of our experience, to have shown how the one continually passes over into the other . . . this is to have presented the *datum* which all our adventures, worldly and otherworldly alike, must take into account. (p. 54)

This is one of the few places in his literary criticism where Lewis has applied what he means by *Sehnsucht* to a given writer's work. In a letter he states that he finds early expressions of this attitude in the *Odyssey,* in Pindar, in some of the choruses of Euripides, in Lucretius' passage about the home of the gods, in the Anglo-Saxon "Seafarer."[4] He is not loath to use his theory of *Sehnsucht* as an instrument of literary analysis. But he recognizes it as a very difficult one to use, because the attitude is so difficult to describe without seeming alternately obscure and obvious, and sometimes even maudlin. All the usual terms of critical discourse mislead by the partiality of their connotations or by the appearance of triteness. In an address given in an Oxford church in 1941, Lewis explains why he believes the emotion remains a nameless one. He says that he feels a certain shyness in speaking of this strange Desire at all, as if he were almost committing an indecency. He refers to it as the "inconsolable secret"

> which hurts so much that you take your revenge on it by calling it names like Nostalgia and Romanticism and Adolescence; the secret also which pierces with such sweetness that when, in very intimate conversation, the mention of it grows imminent, we

[4] Letter to author dated December 10, 1958.

grow awkward and affect to laugh at ourselves; the secret which we cannot hide and cannot tell, though we desire to do both.[5]

Because men can neither hide nor tell this secret they content themselves with identifying its strangely nourishing melancholy with concrete, everyday experiences: books, travel, avocations, friends. Lewis speaks of this in *The Problem of Pain:*

> You may have noticed that the books you really love are bound together by a secret thread. . . . Even in your hobbies, has there not always been some secret attraction which the others are curiously ignorant of—something, not to be identified with, but always on the verge of breaking through, the smell of cut wood in the workshop or the clap-clap of water against the boat's side?

There is often in this sort of experience a joyful moment of discovery:

> Are not all lifelong friendships born when at last you meet another human being who has some inkling (but faint and uncertain even in the best) of that something you were born desiring, and which, beneath the flux of other desires and in all the momentary silences between the louder passions, night and day, year by year, from childhood to old age, you are looking for, watching for, listening for?[6]

Such are some of the everyday manifestations of this strange Desire. But the most common manifestation in the world of workaday reality as well as in the world of fiction and poetry is the conviction that one must undertake a quest, must seek the Well at the World's End, that the seeking will both ease the longing and make of this indeterminate emotion something of significance.

The quest

In his *English Literature in the Sixteenth Century* Lewis has an intriguing comment on Spenser which is another

---

[5] *The Weight of Glory and Other Addresses* (Grand Rapids: Eerdmans, 1965), p. 4.

[6] New York: Macmillan, 1944, pp. 133-134.

instance of his applying the theory of *Sehnsucht* to practical criticism. In speaking of Spenser in Ireland, Lewis quotes Bernard Shaw on what Ireland can do to some minds: "Such colours in the sky . . . such lure in the distances . . . such sadness in the evenings. Oh, the dreaming! the torturing, heartscalding, never satisfying dreaming!" Lewis does not say that Spenser felt this; in fact, he admits that the matter is highly speculative. But he does say that if Spenser had felt such melancholy it would have been appropriate to Arthur's endless quest.[7]

Questing seems to be a logical outgrowth of the sort of opulent melancholy we are dealing with here. For it is melancholy with glimpses of Joy or, put another (equally unsatisfactory) way, it is Joy which is somehow one with the awareness of loss. In *Dymer* Lewis wrote:

> . . . Joy flickers on
> The razor-edge of the present and is gone.
> (p. 51)

And the sense of loss excites interest in the quest. Lewis suggests that this is why human beings cannot enjoy being happy for long. When they are happy they lose sight of the quest and reproach themselves, consciously or not. As Mrs. Dimble says in *That Hideous Strength:* "Do human beings *like* being happy?" She confesses that for some reason she rather enjoys a little melancholy.[8]

In *The Pilgrim's Regress* the idea of the compulsive quest is necessarily bound up with this desirable melancholy which ordinary discourse can only flounderingly describe. At the beginning of the story John is walking along a road when he hears sweet, strange music and a voice which says "Come." Then he suddenly notices a garden wall with a window in it and through the window he sees a greenwood full of primroses. The scene reminds him of something he cannot remember, and while he is trying to grasp what it is, a remarkable thing happens. The

---

[7] *English Literature in the Sixteenth Century* (London: Oxford, 1954), pp. 356-357.

[8] New York: Macmillan, 1946, p. 79.

mist at the end of the wood seems to part and through the rift he sees a calm sea and an island. A sensation of "unbounded sweetness" passes over him and when it is gone he says to himself, " 'I know now what I want.' The first time that he said it, he was aware that it was not entirely true: but before he went to bed he was believing it."[9]

John's desire to find the Island leads him on a long search wherein he first enjoys the body of a voluptuous brown girl (sensuality without meaning)[10] whose voice is sweet but unlike the voice he had heard beside the garden wall. He meets a refined and austere old gentleman named Mr. Halfways (Romantic poetry) who has a daughter named Media. They say that they know about the Island he is seeking and that he must seek it within himself. As he listens to Mr. Halfways sing, he regains his vision of the Island and is about to make love to Media, her father having disappeared, when a solemn-faced youth in wire clothing breaks in upon them. He tells John that all the music and caresses of this place are only a mask for lust. He is a tough-minded devotee of the art of Eschropolis (literary trends in the twenties) and invites John to visit this community of brave realists who have discovered that Romanticism is "all self-deception and phallic sentiment" (p. 47). In Eschropolis John meets the Clevers, who gather in a laboratory to write machine-age verse. They are a thin, sharp-tongued lot who stand about sipping drinks which look like medicines and promptly accuse whoever disagrees with them of being inhibited or impotent. But in spite of their capacity for frank analysis, their kind of art seems to lead also to brown girls—without so much as a glimpse of the Island.

For the rest of the book John journeys from one philosopher to another and tries their suggestions. But he cannot find the Island, though the desire for it frequently returns.

The quest motif is also presented in Lewis' interplane-

9 *The Pilgrim's Regress,* revised edition (Grand Rapids: Eerdmans, 1958), pp. 24-25. All subsequent references are to this revised edition.

10 My identification of the allegorical figures follows Lewis' running headlines for the revised edition.

tary trilogy: *Out of the Silent Planet, Perelandra,* and *That Hideous Strength.* Mythopoeic fiction provides him with a more complete means of working out his ideas than expository prose or even allegory. To use two memorable phrases which Charles Brady has applied to Lewis, "the upland slopes of allegory" are one thing; "the ringing crags of myth"[11] another. Lewis has tried both and he is also one of the most accomplished English essayists, but in actually communicating *Sehnsucht* he is at his best in myth. The many considerations which in the other genres hamper one from fully responding to certain emotions are removed. And the result is exciting; in fact it is hard to imagine quests more exciting than those on which Lewis' characters are embarked in these stories: gold-prospecting on Mars, a trip from earth to Venus in a coffin which sails through the luminous heavens—landing in a gold and emerald sea of floating islands—and a battle against Satanic forces which involves a search for the ancient magician Merlin. No outline conveys anything of the strange beauty and power of these novels. They are often more like prose poems, and yet the suspense of a good story is maintained. The style, especially in *Perelandra,* as Victor Hamm points out, has the Shelleyan "elan and lucidity, and the Shelleyan buoyancy."[12]   There is a mood of almost limitless possibility appropriate to the life of a planet which has not succumbed to evil. And it is precisely this buoyancy which makes me think of these interplanetary adventures as being in themselves an expression of *Sehnsucht.*[13]

Longing on other planets

As Lewis points out in his essay "On Stories," there are tales which both children and adults like to hear over and

11 "Introduction to C. S. Lewis," *America,* May 27, 1944, p. 214.

12 "Mr. Lewis in Perelandra," *Thought: Fordham University Quarterly,* 20 (June, 1945), 271-290.

13 Cf. what Lewis says of the effect of Malacandrian beauty on Ransom: "He felt the old lift of the heart, the soaring solemnity, the sense, at once sober and ecstatic, of life and power offered in unasked and unmeasured abundance"—*Out of the Silent Planet* (New York: Macmillan, 1943), p. 107.

over again even though they know the ending.[14] They are held, he says, by glimpses of the "Other-World," which provide a certain buoyancy, verve, or excitement—call it what you will. Thus by their very nature fairy tales and myths often express the questing desire I have been discussing in this chapter. I will not press the point here; the relation between *Sehnsucht* and myth-making will be explored in Chapter V. There is a danger of course in talking about necessarily ill-defined emotions that all sorts of things will be connected with them. But whatever may be the real connections here, Lewis certainly reflects his concern with *Sehnsucht*, by direct comment, in the interplanetary trilogy.

In *Out of the Silent Planet*, Ransom, a Cambridge philologist, is kidnapped by Weston and Devine, who want to offer him as a human sacrifice to the natives of Mars. These men have perfected a spaceship in order to bring back gold from that planet, though Weston, a Life-Force worshipper, has a "higher" purpose also in wanting to spread human culture throughout the universe. They land on Mars with Ransom as their prisoner, but he escapes and discovers a strange ancient world of purple *handramits* (valleys) and rose-colored forests. He is befriended by its inhabitants, three strange species of rational beings: the *séroni*—tall, lean, man-like creatures with feathered legs, who are the scientists and technologists of Malacandra (the Old Solar name for Mars); the *pfifltriggi*—frog-like workers who make the things the *séroni* devise; and the *hrossa*— lovable penguin-like beings who fish, make poems, and sing songs. In this hierarchical society all the creatures are at peace and their nearest equivalent for the word "evil" is "bent." They lift and dig and carry on their arts with ease. They are specialized but not excessively so. An artist, for example, lives close to the things he wants to depict, and all enjoy one another's talents. The *hrossa*, who are described in terms reminiscent of medieval bestiaries and who speak in a stark poetic style not unlike Old English verse, explain to Ransom their poetry and the religion of

14 *Essays Presented to Charles Williams*, p. 103.

Malacandra. The Cambridge don, being able to understand enough of Old Solar to follow this explanation, discovers among other things that longing is not painful to the *hrossa.* "A pleasure is full grown only when it is remembered," they tell him. Thus the things which come only once in a *hross'* life, such as mating, are not only enjoyed in anticipation but are remembered and "boiled inside," being made later "into poems and wisdom." Ransom finds there are two words for longing: *wondelone,* which refers to the attitude just described, and *bluntheline,* a kind of longing which only "bent" minds engage in (pp. 76-77).

The Malacandrians cannot understand the earth evils which Ransom tells of, for they are happy under the conditions which Maleldil (God) has ordained and can hardly conceive of disobedience. It is clear that they live in a world where the "unbodying" rod of Oyarsa (a tutelary spirit who acts as Maleldil's deputy)[15] permits no evil to grow and thus they do not have free will in any moral sense. Since no one can disobey Oyarsa and long remain in existence, it is inevitable that Weston and Devine should be apprehended in their evil intentions and sent back to earth. Ransom is sent with them as part of his preparation for some future mission.

This mission turns out to be a visit to Venus, which is told in *Perelandra.* Ransom is propelled from earth to this paradise of warm seas and exotic floating islands by the *eldila,* who appear as flickering light and act as the messengers of Maleldil. Ransom does not know why he has been brought to Venus until he discovers that Weston is there also. The bent *eldil* of earth (Satan) has taken possession of the space-travelling physicist Weston and is using him to bring about the corruption of Venus. It is a new planet where a beautiful green lady and her husband live happily, under one constraint from Maleldil—they must not stay overnight on one of the fixed islands. Weston endeavors to beguile the Green Lady into disobeying Mal-

---

15The name "Oyarsa," as Ransom discovers on his return to earth, occurs in its latinized form, *oyarses,* in the work of a twelfth-century Christian Platonist, Bernard of Tours (Silvestris).

eldil. Her husband is away on a hunting expedition and she becomes steadily more impressed with Weston's arguments, in spite of Ransom's rebuttals. Eventually Ransom resorts to physically attacking the demonic agent whose blasphemy has finally transformed him into a horrible creature called the "Un-Man." In the long, gory struggle Ransom finally destroys the Un-Man in an underground cave. Though he is wounded, he is enabled to return to earth for one last mission. A summary of the book inevitably sounds bald beside its actual richness of description and allegorical suggestiveness.

But to the significant point for this discussion: Ransom discovers that on Venus wanting is not painful, at least not for the Green Lady. She has no concept of what disappointment or frustration might be, for she lives in a world where whatever is, is good. In talking with Ransom she discovers that in his world not all events are pleasing or welcome. She begins to understand that when, for example, she goes into the forest to pick fruit and finds a different fruit than the one she had thought of when she set out, her reaction could be like what Ransom is telling her. And yet she feels no disappointment in finding a different fruit; on Perelandra it is simply that one pleasure "was expected and another given." She finally grasps in a dim way what "not-good" would be when she says: "You could send your soul after the good you had expected, instead of turning it to the good you got. You could refuse the real good; you could make the real fruit taste insipid by thinking of the other."[16]

It is by such a gradual process that Ransom tries to explain to the Lady what sorrow and death are in a fallen world and how wanting can be painful. Yet when Ransom tries to illustrate his point by asking her if she is happy without the King, her husband—does she not want him?— she replies: "How could there be anything I did not want?" (p. 69).

Wanting for Ransom, however, involves both melancholy and joy, as it does on earth. The beauty of Pere-

[16] *Perelandra* (New York: Macmillan, 1944), p. 67.

landra (the Old Solar name for Venus) at times almost overwhelms him. On waking one morning he suddenly feels he has dreamed all this beauty, and thoughts of living and walking "on the oceans of the Morning Star" rush "through his memory with a sense of lost sweetness" (p. 100). One night he rides a great silvery fish through the warm breakers and sees heraldic water beasts, among them friendly sea-dragons and sea-centaurs who, by their almost human features, make him feel somehow akin. And the sweet night breezes of Perelandra remind him of the Islands' tranquil beauty by daylight:

> He would know it henceforward out of the whole universe—the night-breath of a floating island in the star Venus. It was strange to be filled with homesickness for places where his sojourn had been so brief and which were, by any objective standard, so alien to all our race. Or were they? The cord of longing which drew him to the invisible isle seemed to him at that moment to have been fastened long, long before his coming to Perelandra. (p. 104)

This "cord of longing"—seemingly archetypal—was "sharp, sweet, wild, and holy, all in one, and in any world where men's nerves have ceased to obey their central desires would doubtless have been aphrodisiac too" (p. 104).

In *That Hideous Strength* Lewis is less concerned with this kind of longing than he is with something which is often related to *Sehnsucht* in his work, the idea of the numinous. So I will reserve my discussion of the third interplanetary novel for Chapter V, in which I deal with Lewis' treatment of the numinous.

Dominant images of longing in Lewis' work

I find in Lewis' fiction and poetry at least four recurring images which convey *Sehnsucht*. A possible explanation for the importance of the first of these is given in *Surprised by Joy*, where Lewis writes that the green Castlereagh Hills which he saw from his nursery windows taught him longing before he was six years old (p. 7). Thus it is not surprising to find descriptions of distant hills in passages where he deals with *Sehnsucht*. In *Dymer* the old wizard who invites men to escape from life into occultist fancies is troubled by the sight of the far-off hills. He tries to shut them out from his view and he kills a lark whose song reminds him, as do the hills, of the wonder and beauty of the everyday real world (pp. 62-63). In *Till We Have Faces* the description of Psyche's gold and amber house among the hills also conveys *Sehnsucht*, though the implication about the natural world is different. While in *Dymer* it is the everyday world which teaches longing, in *Till We Have Faces* the distant hills point to the other world. Throughout the novel it is the distant hills which come closest to representing (as close as does anything earthly) the surrealistic beauty and otherworldly goal to which Psyche is drawn.[17]

Another recurring image which expresses *Sehnsucht* in Lewis' work is the exotic garden. Several early poems reflect what he says in his autobiography of the first awareness of beauty which he can remember—the toy garden that his brother had made of moss, twigs, and flowers.[18] One of the poems in *Spirits in Bondage* tells of the fabled garden of Hesperides, where the three daughters of the evening star guard a golden tree and an ancient dragon lifts up his head for joy at his master's approach. The poet wishes that he might find this pleasant sleepy land which never fears the sun:

> Through the starry hollow
> Of the summer night
> I would follow, follow
> Hesperus the bright,
> To seek beyond the western wave
> His garden of delight.
> ("Hesperus," pp. 93-95)

Another "lotus land" poem in the same collection also speaks of gardens which lie far, far to the West. "The Song

[17] See especially pp. 75-76 of *Till We Have Faces* (Grand Rapids: Wm. B. Eerdmans, 1966).

[18] *Surprised by Joy*, p. 7.

of the Pilgrims" tells of a search for this fabled peaceful place:

> . . . when at last the ivory port we see
> Our hearts shall melt with mere felicity:
> But we shall wake again in gardens bright
> Of green and gold for infinite delight,
> Sleeping beneath the solemn mountains white
> . . . .
> And ever living queens that grow not old
> And poets wise in robes of faerie gold
> Whisper a wild, sweet song that first was told
> Ere God sat down to make the Milky Way.
> (pp. 70-71)

This second image, the exotic garden, is often bound up, as it is here, with a third, the islands of the "Utter East" or the "Utter West" as in "The Landing." This later poem (it appeared in *Punch* in 1948) also tells of a search for the garden of the Hesperides. The sailors sail far, far to the West and finally sight an island; they land and find that the three daughters of Hesperus are only carved images bound about a tree. And instead of apples they find a golden telescope that is turned to the West. The poem concludes:

> There for the second time I saw, remote and perilous—
> Bliss to behold it in the circle of the lens,
> And this time surely the true one   the Hesperides'
> Country which is not men's.

> Hope died . . . rose again . . . flickered and increased in us;
> Strenuous our longing; we re-embarked to find
> That genuine and utter West. Far astern to East of us
> The false hope sank behind.[19]

Sometimes it is not the remote islands of the Utter West but simply an island which acts as an image of *Sehnsucht*. One of the most memorable passages in *Out of the Silent Planet* describes the island of Oyarsa: in a valley entirely surrounded by tall mountains Ransom sees a sapphire-colored lake and an island of pale red which rises from the

<hr/>

[19] "The Landing," published under the pseudonym "N. W.," in *Punch*, 215 (Sept. 15, 1948), 237.

water like a "gently sloping pyramid." And on the summit he sees a grove of trees taller than an earth cathedral spire, which at their top break "rather into flower than foliage, into golden flower bright as tulips, still as rock, and huge as summer cloud" (p. 113). The sight of the Island awakens in Ransom (as it does in John in *The Pilgrim's Regress*) a feeling of mingled awe and desire.

A fourth thing which stimulates longing in Lewis' work is music—not just any sort of music but a very particular kind. In an essay called "Transposition" Lewis discusses a passage in *Pepys' Diary* which describes the kind. Pepys mentions that he heard in a play some sweet music which ravished his soul almost to the point of nausea.[20] In Lewis' work it is this kind of music which conveys *Sehnsucht*—sounds which awake sweet desire at once so fleeting and so overwhelming that one reacts to some degree in this way. An example of such a musical stimulus is found in one of Lewis' stories for children, *The Voyage of the "Dawn Treader,"* which uses all the dominant images of *Sehnsucht* I have discussed here. It is a story of a quest for the "Utter East," which involves an exciting voyage for three English children aboard a ship called the "Dawn Treader." They travel with strange chivalric animals and medieval noblemen, and have many fantastic adventures which recall the fiction of Jonathan Swift and George Macdonald: a visit to a land of invisible people, the discovery of a magic book which shows pictures of whatever one thinks as he reads it, the finding of a castle where three men have been sleeping about a banquet table for so long that their hair and beards entirely cover them. But the climax of their adventures comes when the "Dawn Treader" sails at last into the flower-covered seas at the very end of the world. Here the water is sweet, and when the company drink of it they feel "almost too well and strong to bear it."[21] They need no food and can stare at the sun. A sweet breeze comes out of the East and with it a musical sound.

[20] *The Weight of Glory and Other Addresses*, p. 19.
[21] *The Voyage of the "Dawn Treader"* (New York: Macmillan, 1952), p. 194.

Edmund and Eustace would never talk about it afterwards. Lucy could only say, "It would break your heart." "Why," said I, "was it so sad?"—"Sad!! No," said Lucy. No one in the boat doubted that they were seeing beyond the End of the World into Aslan's Country.[22]

Narnia in some ways anticipates Heaven. Monarchy and hierarchy are a natural part of its life. Narnian time is different from Earth time, perhaps closer to eternity. Aslan is honored there. Yet it is not Heaven. Aslan's country lies beyond the End of the World and as beautiful and fulfilling as some experiences may be in Narnia, they are but harbingers of Aslan's country.

It is amazing what Lewis is able to do theologically with these seven "stories for children." Kilby believes that if nothing else of Lewis survives in the next century, these tales will and that they will do their share toward undermining the flat secularism of our time. For anyone who wants to see these books opened up so that their riches may be seen but not spoiled, I recommend Walter Hooper's fine essay "Past Watchful Dragons" in *Imagination and the Spirit*, edited by Charles Huttar (Grand Rapids: Eerdmans, 1971), and Kathryn Lindskoog's *The Lion of Judah in Never-Never Land* (Eerdmans, 1973).

The world of faerie

Although we associate fairy tales with children, *faerie* is probably the most complex conveyor of the *Sehnsucht* archetype. And compared to those things which convey *Sehnsucht* discussed earlier—quests, distant hills, exotic gardens, the Utter East, music of a special kind—the world of faerie is perhaps the most potent awakener of longing. Lewis says it stirs and troubles the child, to his advantage, "with the dim sense of something beyond his reach and far from dulling or emptying the actual world, gives it a new dimension of depth" (*Of Other Worlds* [New York: Harcourt Brace, 1966], p. 29).

---

[22] *Ibid.*, p. 206. Aslan is a great lion who acts as the children's protector and guide in all the Narnia books. What he represents will be discussed in Chapter VI.

Lewis is in good company here. Carl Jung, George Macdonald, Richard LeGallienne, G. K. Chesterton, and J. R. R. Tolkien have all written convincingly on the sanity and goodness of the world of faerie.[23] Fairy tales can be Christian without being parochial, moral without being rationalistic or hortatory, shining with goodness, wonder, and love without being in the least sentimental. Yet, as Chesterton observes, the action may seem amazingly arbitrary:

> The vision always hangs upon a veto. . . . An incomprehensible happiness rests upon an incomprehensible condition. A box is opened, and all evils fly out. A word is forgotten, and cities perish. A lamp is lit, and love flies away. A flower is plucked, and human lives are forfeited. An apple is eaten, and the hope of God is gone.[24]

As Lewis points out in "On Stories," a child asks for the same fairy story again and again, even when he knows the outcome, because he wants the glimpse of faerie—what Tolkien has called the "piercing glimpse of joy, and heart's desire" ("On Fairy Stories," pp. 81-82 in *Essays Presented to Charles Williams*).

It is as if faerie is the fifth column of the Supernatural (or the Arch-natural, as Charles Williams called it), which works against neat rationalisms and dulling conventions—to keep wonder alive in us. For adults today the faerie recrudesces in romantic films and fiction, advertising images, travel, and furtive amours. These are very impure forms of the faerie but close to it whenever they promote a disinterested dreaming and the thrill of stepping into another world.

People simply cannot live without the dimension of wonder. It may well be that someday we will become convinced that it was the combination of city life, machinery, and a social-science-dominated education which drove many young people to drugs, in the sixties especially. For a young person, overburdened with current

[23] See James Higgins, *Beyond Words: Mystical Fancy in Children's Literature* (New York: Teachers College Press, 1970) for an excellent discussion of the sanity of faerie.

[24] *Orthodoxy* (Garden City: Garden City Publ., 1908), 290-291.

events, pressured to compete and succeed, out of touch with nature and his own body, and steeped in books about how food gets into New York and how the fire department and the electoral college work, there *must* be some ecstatic escape. And if he is an American it is natural to "solve" the problem with a pill.

The great interest young people currently have in Tolkien, Lewis, and other "fantasy" writers provides additional evidence of a felt need.[25]

As William Morris' evocation of "Joy" drew Lewis through Paganism to Christianity, so in the future many who are now young will discover some of the Old Western values and perhaps even Christian belief through the world of fantasy and faerie.

The significance of "Joy-Melancholy" in Lewis' work

In all his work Lewis, like Dr. Johnson, is always the moralist. He is of course too accomplished an artist ever to engage in pedestrian moralizing. Yet his stories, poems, and essays have deeply moral implications which the reader can hardly avoid. Those who pick up *Out of the Silent Planet* or *Perelandra* expecting only a good escape story or read a poem expecting only to be entertained may feel that they have been "tricked" into facing issues and questions which they might prefer not to face. Lewis rejects literary snobbery and sees no reason why one's reading should not be entertaining, but he wants to make no concessions to entertainment-seekers which would falsify life or present it as something less than the complex, mysterious thing that it is. His readers will find interesting story (and acceptable verse), but they will also have to look at human experience, for a little while at least, with a willingness to see in it some of the wonder and "soul-size" implications which Lewis has seen.

What he says of that indeterminate "Joy-Melancholy" which Tillyard speaks of will baffle some readers and

---

25 For a profound discussion of the loss of transcendence see Nathan A. Scott's *The Broken Center*, especially ch. 5 (New Haven: Yale, 1966).

94

excite others. For those who are set to thinking about the significance of this emotion, he provides no easy definitions or answers. To be sure, the experience at times sounds like the symptoms of acute neurasthenia, as in "The Day With the White Mark":

> . . . I could have kissed the very scullery taps.
>
>   The color of
> My day was like a peacock's chest.
> . . . .
> So everything, the tick of the clock, the cock
>
>   crowing in the yard,
> Probing my soil, woke diverse buried hearts of
>
>   mine to beat.[26]

And Dymer, in his remote land not unlike ancient Greece, is no stranger to another psychological explanation, the wish-fulfillment theory. He wonders if the object of sweet desire is after all only the mirror of his heart, "Such things as boyhood feigns beneath the smart / Of solitude and spring."[27] If melancholy mingled with joy were all, perhaps some of the psychological theories about overstimulated nerves and the recrudescence of puberty would seem more satisfactory. But there is another important human response involved with this complex of emotions Lewis calls *Sehnsucht*—man's awareness of the numinous. Lewis believes that *Sehnsucht* has an *object,* and his interpretation of what that object is must be understood in the light of what he sees as the connection between "primal Joy-Melancholy" and the numinous.

[26] *Punch,* 217 (Aug. 17, 1949), 170.
[27] *Dymer,* p. 78.

V BRITAIN AND LOGRES.
Nature and Arch-nature

The unintelligible forms of ancient poets
The fair humanities of old religion,
The power, the beauty, and the majesty,
That had their haunts in dale or piny mountain,
. . . .
. . . all these have vanished.
They live no longer in the faith of reason.
But still the heart doth need a language, still
Doth the old instinct bring back the old names.
—Coleridge (adapting Schiller)

In *The Personal Heresy* Lewis says that he believes there
are two kinds of poetry. The first deals with experiences
which all men have, is what the classicists would call a
"just representation of general nature." The second gives a
"new and nameless sense," provides an experience which
nothing in the everyday business of living would prepare
one for. Lewis finds this quality of strangeness in only a
few poets: occasionally in Virgil, in the later works of
Shakespeare, in Blake, Morris, George Macdonald, Poe, and
T. S. Eliot (pp. 102-103). This nameless sense is, I believe,
closely related to the idea of the numinous, which, as I
have pointed out in Chapter I, communicates a sense of
disorientation in the face of awesome mystery much as
Sehnsucht communicates a sense of disorientation in
melancholy or questing.

The idea of the numinous long interested Lewis; indeed it was instrumental in his conversion to Christianity. Rudolf Otto's *The Idea of the Holy*, which explores the philosophical implications of this strange sense, made a profound impression on Lewis in the 1920's, and he has since drawn upon Otto's work, particularly in *The Problem of Pain*. Although he does not accept all of Otto's thesis, he does believe that the notion of religious awe as something apart from rational deduction, morality, and aesthetic response is a valid one. Danger and fear, Lewis says in *The Problem of Pain*, are not enough to awaken the sense of the numinous. One's response, for example, to the idea of a tiger in the next room is quite different from one's response to the idea of a ghost or a Great Spirit in the next room (p. 5). There is in the experience of the numinous an awareness of the uncanny and a dread of the power behind it—something not to be inferred, as fear is, from physical facts and logical deductions about them. Lewis thus believes that this sense of the numinous, expressed in dread and awe, is in "a different dimension from fear," is "in the nature of an interpretation" which we give to the universe (p. 8).

In the interplanetary novels man's sense of his own finiteness and his awe in the presence of "supernatural" power are expressed with great force. Ransom in *Out of the Silent Planet* looks through a telescope on Mars and sees earth—a whirling disk, yet "it was all there . . . London, Athens, Jerusalem, Shakespeare . . . and his pack . . . still lying in the porch of an empty house near Sterk" (p. 103). And when he is aboard the spaceship journeying back to earth, he cannot feel that it is "an island of life journeying through an abyss of death." He feels instead that life is all around them waiting to break in and that if it kills them it would do so by "excess of its vitality" (p. 159). In *Perelandra* Ransom senses the presence of Maleldil, which makes darkness seem "packed quite full" and light brighter and denser; he realizes that since coming to Venus he has been continually aware of a kind of pressure about him, so gentle it could be ignored yet occasionally so strong its existence is undeniable (pp. 145-146).

But Lewis' most extended treatment of the numinous in fiction is in the third book of the interplanetary trilogy, *That Hideous Strength*. Its story is different from the other two in that all the action takes place on earth. Yet the novel is concerned with earth in two different sets of dimensions: the mundane, everyday, geographical world, and the spiritual world where the battle between good and evil reveals the everyday reality to be only a pale backdrop for the action of the drama. This, however, is not immediately clear to most of the characters, and *That Hideous Strength* tells how several people come to discover the authenticity of "unseen" things.[1] The two main characters are Mark Studdock, an ambitious but confused young man who holds a fellowship in sociology at Bracton College, and his wife Jane. They are typical of the debunking, somewhat cynically sophisticated intellectuals in the aftermath of two World Wars, disillusioned and without any consistent system of values. They believe in freedom, independence, and a tough-minded, scientific approach to life—so much so that their marriage has little meaning. Because of his interest in using science to improve society, Mark investigates a position with the N. I. C. E. (the National Institute of Co-ordinated Experiments). This is a sinister group of power-hungry men who want to gain control of England and eventually the whole world in order that scientifically controlled progress may rid the earth of superstition, dirt, and disease. At least this is what the merely misguided among them believe. Actually the inner group, led by Frost and Wither, are in league with demonic forces called "macrobes," which speak through Alcasan, a murderer whose guillotined head they have managed by ingenious means to keep alive.

The "macrobes," led by the Bent Eldil of earth (Satan),

---

[1] In *The Screwtape Letters* the senior tempter explains that one of the chief tasks of his kind is to keep the attention of human beings focused on the mundane and the everyday. Once, he says, "a patient, a sound atheist, who used to read in the British Museum" began to pursue a line of thought which brought the Enemy (God) to his side. But Screwtape quickly got him out of the library, showed him "a newsboy shouting the midday paper, and a No. 73 bus going past"—this "healthy dose of 'real life' " being enough to chase thoughts of the Enemy clean away (New York: Macmillan, 1943), pp. 13-14.

direct the N. I. C. E. in their "glorious" purpose of creating a new kind of human being, one that will be completely obedient to the evil powers. All of the totalitarian methods are used: the press is corrupted, vicious propaganda is circulated, "truth" becomes what is useful to the cause, torture and secret police are used to hold people in the organization and make them conform to the will of the leaders. Thus Mark Studdock becomes a prisoner of the N. I. C. E. before he knows it, and begins to experience the great pressure of demonic forces upon his whole being.

Thus far the story reads like an anticipation of Orwell's *1984.*[2] The great difference between Orwell's novel and *That Hideous Strength* is that in the latter a great counterforce emerges to combat the formidable power of evil. In the quiet manor house of St. Anne's in Edgestow, the city where the N. I. C. E. has its headquarters, a small group of people collect, apparently by accident. They are rather serious in their practice of Christianity, and one by one they have become aware of the gigantic evil which is seeking control of Edgestow. A man named Ransom (the same who voyaged to Mars and Venus) serves as their leader. While Mark is away at N. I. C. E. headquarters, Jane discovers through this group that her troubling dreams actually reveal the plans and operations of the evil organization. Its leaders are trying to get control of her through her husband so that they can use her gift of "second sight" to discover the whereabouts of the ancient magician Merlin. But Jane joins the group at St. Anne's, and through her, contact is made with Merlin. He appears suddenly and acts in behalf of the Christians at St. Anne's to put an end to the evil plottings of the N. I. C. E.

There are two climaxes in the novel; the one at St. Anne's precedes that at Belbury. Before Merlin intervenes he is Ransom's guest for an evening, and on this night the Holy Ghost descends on St. Anne's. Most of the company sit quietly in the kitchen, having tea, while upstairs Ransom and Merlin talk. Suddenly the house seems to be

---

[2] A few similarities are so striking that one might see at first some debt in Orwell to Lewis' novel, but I suspect that both writers are influenced by Huxley's *Brave New World*.

moving like a ship on rough water. But there is no fear—
only merriment. A stranger would have thought them
drunk, "not soddenly, but gaily drunk." They were talking, some in rollicking "intellectual duel," with eloquence
and melody, with "skyrockets of metaphor and allusion."
Ransom feels himself "sitting in the very heart of language
. . . . All fact was broken, splashed into cataracts, caught,
turned inside out, kneaded, slain, and reborn as meaning.
For the lord of Meaning himself . . . was with them" (pp.
380-381).

When the orgy of speaking had come to an end, a warm
breeze of indescribable richness came through all the windows and

> a soft tingling as of foam and breaking bubbles ran over their
> flesh. Tears ran down Ransom's cheeks. He alone knew from
> what seas and what islands that breeze blew. Merlin did not; but
> in him also the inconsolable wound with which man is born
> waked and ached at this touching. . . . These yearnings and
> fondlings were however only the fore-runners of the goddess. (p.
> 383)

Then the goddess came (Lewis calls her Charity)—"fiery,
sharp, bright and ruthless, ready to kill, ready to die,
outspeeding light: . . . they were blinded, scorched, deaf-
ened [yet] . . . they could not bear that it should cease"
(p. 383). This baptism of fire prepares the company at St.
Anne's for the final conflict with Belbury. They send
Merlin, imbued with power by this visitation, to N. I. C. E.
headquarters.

The description of what happens there, like the descent
of the gods to St. Anne's, is truly remarkable writing. A
banquet for the members of the N. I. C. E. is turned into
Babel; their speech is so chaotically confused that they
cannot meet any emergency. Then Armageddon begins.
Those who were banqueting are trampled by animals of all
sorts who pay not the slightest heed to these babbling
creatures. A few of the leaders retreat to the underground
vault where Alcasan's head is kept. There—naked, ridicu-
lously obscene, and maniacal—they worship the head and
then proceed to sacrifice one another to it. The last to

remain alive tries to flee but is killed by a huge bear which has discovered the underground chamber. An earthquake swallows up the entire headquarters of the N. I. C. E., and Mark Studdock, unharmed but dazed, makes his way to St. Anne's.

The whole experience has purged both Mark and Jane of the struggle for independence and the attitude of cynical detachment which had plagued their marriage. The novel ends with another remarkable passage in which, after wise words from Ransom, there begin revels of song and dance among all at St. Anne's, including the animals. On this night Mark and Jane enter into a union which will be fruitful because it now has meaning and also because from it will be born a child who will carry on the work of Ransom and the others.

Arch-nature and the numinous

What, in all this, of the numinous? The key is given in an explanation by Dr. Dimble, one of the company which opposes the N. I. C. E. Dimble tells the group that the struggle against evil forces is nothing new in Britain, that it is a country which has always been haunted by "Logres." He uses the name King Arthur gave to the kingdom he wrested from the control of evil spirits as a symbol of a spiritual realm. Dimble explains further that the haunting of Britain by Logres inevitably produces an ambivalent, paradoxical situation: "Haven't you noticed that we are two countries? After every Arthur, a Mordred; behind every Milton, a Cromwell; a nation of poets, a nation of shopkeepers; the home of Sidney—and of Cecil Rhodes" (p. 369).

Logres is perceived in Britain always when men respond to that which comes from "without," inspiring awe, mystery, an awareness of something holy. Logres represents the impingement of the supernatural, not in any simple two-story world but rather in a world where the two kinds of reality "co-inhere."[3] Thus for Lewis as for Charles

[3] For Lewis as for Charles Williams there can be no clear-cut separation between flesh and spirit, between the natural and the supernatural. They exist

51998

Williams (and for Plato) the Real is not *ganz anders* but the archetype of the Phenomenal. Williams in fact coined the term "arch-nature" to avoid the misleading implications of "super-nature." The Divine Majesty is not off in the cloudless heavens. He is here too, and when He makes Himself felt among men, they characterize the experience as belonging to the numinous.

For Lewis and for Charles Williams as well there is something related to the numinous in any real city. For the city presupposes that people have come together on account of values which go beyond mere convenience and the serving of animal needs. There is a sense of destiny and *communitas.* The "polis" has arch-natural overtones in ancient Greece, in Augustine, in the cathedral town, in Renaissance Italy, right down to twentieth-century London. Logres is the city at its best. (See Charles Moorman's *The Precincts of Felicity: The Augustinian City of the Oxford Christians.*)

The key to the city is, in Williams' terms, Exchange. This Exchange may be on the commercial level including the smallest purchase in which one gives to another his attention, smile, small talk, and money; and the other gives some object or service along with his own pleasantries. And this Exchange also involves bearing one another's burdens, as Williams describes the process in his novel *Descent Into Hell.* The Exchange of the City is filled with the sublime and the mundane.

In *That Hideous Strength* the ambiguous relation of the everyday to Arch-nature is quite evident at St. Anne's. Dimble and his wife, Jane Studdock, Denniston, and the others are garden-variety people. Yet under the leadership of Ransom they become convinced of the reality of the unseen country, Logres, to which their deepest allegiance

---

in a kind of broken, paradoxical unity. In man's nature animal and spirit "co-inhere" in such a way that we laugh about our animal functions and yet regard the disembodied spirit (or ghost) with fear (*Miracles,* p. 154).

The concept of co-inherence is also the basis for a related idea found in Lewis and Williams, the doctrine of Substituted Love. Just as flesh and spirit co-inhere, so mankind is bound in a mystical unity, and one often suffers for another. See p. 114 fn. and p. 115 below.

belongs. They are not especially credulous or unstable; in fact, the dour Scotsman McPhee feels it his duty to perform the skeptic's function in discovering truth. He questions them sharply about the N. I. C. E. and about their belief in the miraculous. He discovers, however, that this group regards miracle not as a breaking of law but rather as a divine power working according to its own logic, which, seen from man's point of view, may appear to violate the uniformity of nature.[4] Actually, Denniston observes, there is only a good average uniformity in nature; it is not complete.[5]

The divine "intervention" does not operate according to any of man's standardized notions of how it ought to operate. As Dimble says:

> There are universal rules to which all goodness must conform. But that's only the grammar of virtue. It's not there where the sap is. He doesn't make two blades of grass the same: how much less two saints, two nations, two angels. The whole work of healing Tellus [Earth] depends on nursing that little spark, on incarnating that ghost, which is still alive in every real people, and different in each. When Logres really dominates Britain, when the goddess Reason, the divine clearness, is really enthroned in France, when the order of Heaven is really followed in China—why, then it will be spring. But meantime, our concern is with Logres. (*That Hideous Strength,* p. 444)

The great danger is that Logres will sink into "mere Britain," will become only a nation of commerce-worshippers and debunking intellectuals who believe man is the measure of all things and that "empirical" facts give the final word on human significance and destiny.

---

[4] Cf. what the *séroni* in *Out of the Silent Planet* (pp. 100-101) tell Ransom of the nature of reality: "Body is movement. If it is at one speed, you smell something; if at another, you hear sound; if at another, you see a sight; if at another, you neither see nor hear nor smell, nor know the body in any way." This explanation, similar to recent thinking in physics (i.e., the electronic theory), suggests how Lewis would account for the inadequacy of the scientific method to explain or examine some "unseen" realities. They are at another speed.

[5] *That Hideous Strength*, p. 440. The ideas here are laid out more carefully in a series of lectures called *The Abolition of Man*.

Thus *That Hideous Strength* gives one of Lewis' most forceful attacks on Naturalism—the doctrine, as he defines it, "that only Nature—the whole interlocked system—exists."[6] Christian theology, on the other hand, has generally maintained that the Basic Fact is not Nature but God, that His existence cannot be proved or explained because He is "the ground or starting-point" of all explanations.[7] Moreover (and this is where the idea of the supernatural necessarily enters in), because God exists on His own, He is "on a different level from"[8] all else (Nature), for the existence of all else is contingent upon Him. Lewis believes only supernaturalists see Nature, just as the Latinity of Latin is more evident to modern Englishmen than it was to the Romans.

Therefore the numinous is for Lewis an impingement of that which is not explicable in Naturalistic terms—not explicable, that is, unless one accepts some such theory as that advanced by Freud: that all men inherit an unconscious memory of the death of a prehistoric tribal chief, and the fear and insecurity caused by that event explain this innate dread or sense of alienation from something unseen.

Critical reaction to the trilogy

That Hideous Strength is a potent novel philosophically, and it is potent also in its reworking of Arthurian materials.[9] But at times, as Anne Fremantle observed in her review of the book, the "whole fantasy, gigantic as it is, seems hardly heavyweight enough for the implications."[10] Indeed Lewis is attempting so much here that occasionally the juxtaposition of symbolism and melodramatic detail confuses the reader and gives the impression of floundering bathos. Theodore Spencer found it the least successful of

6 *Miracles*, p. 23.

7 *Ibid.*, p. 17.

8 *Of Other Worlds*, p. 80.

9 See Nathan Comfort Starr, *King Arthur Today* (Gainesville: University of Florida, 1954), pp. 181-188.

10 *New York Herald Tribune Weekly Book Review*, June 2, 1946, p. 12.

the trilogy.[11]   I cannot quite concur with that judgment, for I feel that it must be judged primarily as a separate work, distinctly different in manner and intention from the earlier novels. It lacks the homogeneity of *Out of the Silent Planet* and the soaring lyricism of *Perelandra,* for here Lewis is concerned not with another world beyond the earth but with a world within this world. In *That Hideous Strength* Lewis is attempting to do something which highlights his view of the function of myth.

There is a wide variety of opinion about the comparative success of the three novels in the space-time trilogy, arising, I believe, out of differing tastes in myth-making. Marjorie Hope Nicholson calls *Out of the Silent Planet* the most beautiful voyage novel ever written. R.J. Reilly and also Mark Hillegas, writing in *Shadows of Imagination,* regard it as the most successful of the trilogy. The coherence of this first novel is greater mostly because Lewis is not reaching for as much here as in the other two.

Perelandra is more ambitious, for it is a prose poem, similar in many ways to *Paradise Lost.* (It is interesting that Lewis was working on his *Preface to Paradise Lost* at the time he wrote *Perelandra.*) On Perelandra and in Milton's Eden, nature is good and man lives in harmony with it. The beasts are friendly and subservient to man. Paradise is inhabited by a single couple. Woman is related to man as man is related to God. And God deals with his people directly, imposing one prohibition. Almost all critics have praise for *Perelandra* (it is Kilby's favorite), though Dabney Hart complains that its world never comes to life as Malacandra does because the characters conduct too many dialogues on theology (*C. S. Lewis' Defence of Poesie,* p. 225). Robert Plank in his essay in *Shadows of Imagination* finds in *Perelandra* descriptive parallels to Aldous Huxley's *Doors of Perception,* as if the novel might have been written under the influence of hallucigens. There is no evidence that it was and it seems important to note that Lewis demonstrates here that a person whose

[11] Theodore Spencer, "Symbols of a Good and Bad England," *New York Times Book Review,* July 7, 1946, p. 10.

imagination is keenly developed can have profoundly sensuous mental experiences without drugs.

That Hideous Strength is more often praised and blamed than perhaps any of Lewis' books. Dabney Hart voices an objection similar to Anne Fremantle's, that the story is not substantial enough to support the mythic and symbolic load with which Lewis weights it. Yet it is my favorite novel by Lewis and the favorite part of the trilogy for Nathan Comfort Starr and Charles Moorman.

Lewis as mythmaker

It is significant, I believe, that in all of Lewis' fiction and most of his poetry, particularly those works in which he seeks to communicate *Sehnsucht,* he makes use either of allegory or of what we may call mythopoeic art. As early as the 1930's, when he was writing *The Allegory of Love,* he had come to regard allegory as a form which not only reflects psychological conflicts but which often reveals profound metaphysical assumptions. Allegory to Lewis is more than a sugar coating on the moral pill. He says that it was not meant to be a "mere device, or figure of rhetoric, or fashion, "though at times it may become such.

> On the contrary, it was originally forced into existence by a profound moral revolution occurring in the latter days of paganism. For reasons of which we know nothing at all—here again the "seminal form" not to be explained by history—man's gaze was turned inward . . . [in order that man might describe] the contending forces which cannot be described at all except by allegory.[12]

Lewis used allegory in *The Pilgrim's Regress* and in *The Great Divorce,* both of which employ two basic devices of traditional allegory, the dream-vision and the journey. But neither of these works is as good as his interplanetary trilogy, the Narnia series, and *Till We Have Faces,* all of which, though they have allegorical elements, may more properly be called myths. In allegory there is a rough

[12] *The Allegory of Love,* p. 113.

one-to-one relation between fictional character, place, or situation and some abstract entity (love, pride, despair). In myth the relation between imagery and metaphysics or ethics is more complex. One cannot go through the story saying this means this and that means that. But both myth and allegory create worlds of their own, somewhat unrealistic perhaps by the standards of conventional fiction but worlds which have nonetheless a powerful psychological or surrealistic validity.[13]

Unfortunately the word "myth" usually suggests something which did not happen or could not have happened. Lewis, along with most other literary scholars, objects to thinking of myth in this way. For him the great myths of the Bible as well as of pagan literature refer not to the nonhistorical but rather to the nondescribable.[14] The historical correlative for something like the Genesis account of the creation and fall of man may be disputed. But the theological validity of the myth rests on its uniqueness as an account of real creation (out of nothing), on its psychological insight into the rebellious will of man, and on its clear statement that man has a special dignity by virtue of his being made in God's "image." Only a story such as this can address the reader in several dimensions at once: psychological and theological as well as aesthetic.

Thus in Lewis' understanding of myth the story outline is analogous to the metaphor in poetry. (In fact, he says in *The Allegory of Love* that "every metaphor is an allegory in little"—p. 60.) There is a danger of course in coming to regard such a story literally (e. g., trying to visualize God making Eve from one of Adam's bones). But this is an

[13] Cf. Lewis' comments in his introduction to the anthology of MacDonald's work: "It [myth] is in some ways more akin to music than to poetry—or at least to most poetry. It goes beyond expression of things we have already felt. It arouses in us sensations we have never had before, never anticipated having, as though we had broken out of our normal mode of consciousness and 'possessed joys not promised to our birth.' It gets under our skin, hits us at a level deeper than our thoughts or even our passions, troubles oldest certainties till all questions are re-opened, and in general shocks us more fully awake than we are for most of our lives" (pp. 16-17).

[14] See *Miracles*, pp. 95-97.

inescapable danger, as Lewis explains in an essay on metaphor:

> When we pass beyond pointing to individual sensible objects, when we begin to think of causes, relations, of mental states or acts, we become incurably metaphorical. We apprehend none of these things except through metaphor. . . . Our only choice is to use the metaphors and thus to think something, though less than we could wish; or else to be driven by unrecognized metaphors [especially so-called "scientific" language which pretends to be literal when no language can be completely so] and so think nothing at all. I myself would prefer to embrace the former choice.[15]

Myth then points to realities which simply cannot be discussed in literal language. To speak within the context of Lewis' thought, one could say that such stories are inspired by "Arch-nature" impinging upon "Nature" and that whenever "Arch-nature" is seen clearly, it stimulates men to make tales which have the singular fantastic quality which we associate with myth. Thus Ransom thinks ruefully that when he returns to earth all the things he has experienced on Malacandra will seem like mythology. "It even occurred to him that the distinction between history and mythology might be itself meaningless outside the Earth."[16] The suggestion is that maybe the dichotomy between mythology and history is a result of living in a fallen world. It does not follow, however, that history is necessarily a falsification of reality or that all myths are true simply because they are myths. In *The Regress* Wisdom tells John that there is a divinely appointed mythology which was given to the "shepherd people," yet from a literary point of view, it partakes of many of the characteristics of any mythology.[17]

As Wayne Shumaker observed, myth-making has been much talked about in recent years but Lewis was one of

[15] "Bluspels and Flalansferes," *Rehabilitations*, p. 154.

[16] *Out of the Silent Planet*, pp. 156-157. A similar observation is made in *Perelandra*, p. 149.

[17] Cf. *Miracles*, p. 161, fn.

the few writers to attempt anything in this genre.[18] Perhaps this general failure among writers to do much with myth is symptomatic of the spirit of an age which has developed a thoroughly Naturalistic view of the world. Certainly there have been few if any great mythical poems since *Faust* or *The Nibelung's Ring*,[19] and it may be that only with the demise of a scientific Naturalism run amuck, will it again be possible for many writers to see the world as a vast stage where mighty forces, from within and without, contend for man's soul. Lewis' use of myth is indeed the opposite of the use made by James Joyce and other modern writers who seize on myth to give some kind of form to the chaos of experience. Lewis believes, instead, that in its imaginative appeal the myth conveys meaning that cannot be conveyed in any other way. He believes that meaning and myth are inextricably bound up so that one cannot simply impose a myth on experience if he is going to be true to the reality of the myth.

Though he favors a systematic view of the world, Lewis does not find this a cozy universe. He says that in it we can find some love, some merriment, and some feeling of success in our work, but—if we are honest—not much snug, settled happiness.[20] Reality is far too terrifying, ecstatic, and mysterious for that. The domestic irony of a Jane Austen or a Trollope can create telling miniatures so long as it is confined to the tamer realities. In such writers we learn a good deal of ourselves, with unquestioned delight, but for awe, majesty, unquenchable longing, we must look to a different kind of literature, particularly to the myth.

In his *Experiment in Criticism* Lewis says that in a myth a man "puts what he does not yet know and could not come by in any other way."[21] He also points out that all descriptions of reality are mythic when they purport to be

[18] "The Cosmic Trilogy of C. S. Lewis," *The Hudson Review*, 8 (Summer, 1955), 240-254.

[19] Lewis would add Shelley's *Prometheus*. See "Dryden, Shelley, and Mr. Eliot," *Rehabilitations*, p. 30.

[20] *The Problem of Pain*, p. 103.

[21] New York: Cambridge, 1961, p. 41.

absolute truth, so even in our secular age we have the Marxist myth, the Freudian myth, the scientism myth, etc. Myth appears to have its own inner life, secret from our conscious minds. (This idea supports Barfield's belief in the superiority of primitive man's kind of relatedness to the world.)

According to Tolkien, myth "is alive at once and in all its parts, and dies before it can be dissected" (*Beowulf: the Monsters and the Critics*, pp. 256-257). The teller of the story is in some sense floating on a stream which has its own currents. He is not wholly in charge but can paddle in the stream, directing his boat toward a particular destination. That modern men continue to make myths gives support to many of Jung's theories and suggests we will not settle for the secular vision that this world is all there is.

Lewis' preference for mythic art is bound up with his awareness of the power, even terror, of the battle between good and evil. What Nathan Starr has said of Charles Williams might be said also of Lewis:

> To him evil is a spiritual reality; it is not caused by a dislocation of genes or hormones or a set of psychopathic fixations. It is a gigantic negative force aimed at the reduction of the cosmos ordained by the Divine Will, and it operates through the degradation of fallible human beings.[22]

And the most profoundly strange thing about evil is its often ambiguous relation to good. In *Out of the Silent Planet* one of the *hrossa* tells Ransom of that which most closely parallels evil in an unfallen world. This is the *hnakra*, a large, shining water-beast, which often tries to kill the *hrossa* and whose nearness can make rational creatures morally "bent." But so long as they relentlessly seek out these beasts and kill them, they have nothing to fear. In fact, the *hross* explains: "I do not think the forest would be so bright, nor the water so warm, nor love so sweet, if there were no danger in the lakes."[23]   In Lewis'

---

[22] *King Arthur Today*, p. 165.

[23] *Out of the Silent Planet*, p. 79. Although Lewis sees an ambiguous relation between good and evil in the natural world, it is necessary to add

thought danger is the result of freedom. Neither is evil in itself but because both are necessary for genuine good, both are also potential sources of evil.

Surreality in Till We Have Faces

Lewis' most subtle treatment of the relation between good and evil is found in his last novel, *Till We Have Faces*, which also has powerful numinous elements. It is based on Apuleius' tale of Cupid and Psyche, yet the story which emerges is quite different. Orual, the eldest daughter of the King of Glome, writes her case against the gods, and her story is so convincing that Apuleius' tale appears to be an involuntary corruption of the original story. (This view of the Psyche story would of course be compatible with Lewis' belief that most myths were originally theological in import.)

The setting is a semi-barbaric kingdom in southern Europe or southwest Asia; the time is vaguely set at some period between the fourth and first centuries B.C. Orual's mother being dead, the king remarries in order to beget a male heir. His new wife dies in giving birth to yet another daughter, named Istra, and Orual, though still a girl, takes the child to raise as her own. Istra (also called Psyche) becomes as beautiful as a goddess and is greatly loved of the people. Yet when plague comes and rumors of enemy attack threaten Glome, the priest of the House of Ungit says that Psyche must be given to the god of the Mountain, who is (to speak "in a mystery") Ungit's husband and also her son (p. 55). Psyche faces her death unafraid, for she has often dreamed of a gold and amber house in the mountains and believes that the god of the Mountain has long been wooing her (p. 76). Orual is hurt and puzzled at her half-sister's willingness to leave her. But she becomes even more disturbed when, some days after Psyche is tied

---

quickly here that in *The Great Divorce* he has written of the dangers of glossing over the distinctions between good and evil when one is confronted with a moral decision. "Good, as it ripens, becomes continually more different" from evil. Many situations do present us with unavoidable either-or's. See the preface to *The Great Divorce*.

to the tree of the Accursed and left for the god of the
Mountain, Orual discovers she is living in a valley beyond
the holy tree. Her joy at seeing radiantly alive the one
whose bones she has come to bury is soon turned to sorrow.
For Psyche refuses to return with her sister. She says that
she now lives in her husband's palace and invites Orual to
ascend the great stairs. She tells her that although her
husband comes to her only in the darkness and that, in
accordance with his wish, she has never seen him, she loves
him greatly. She shows Orual the royal robes which he has
given her. Orual sees only the rags of Psyche's funeral dress
and an empty valley.

But that evening, camped beside the river which sep-
arates Psyche's dwelling-place from the rest of Glome,
Orual drinks from the stream and raises her head to see,
gray and motionless on the other side, "a labyrinthine
beauty . . . of pillar and arch and architrave"—for a moment, Psyche's palace—and then only fog (p. 132). Briefly
Orual too believes that Psyche is the bride of the god of
the Mountain. But the thought that someone else should
have the beautiful sister who is all that Orual has missed
being is too much. She wants to see the palace, but she
cannot give Psyche up. She resolves that it shall be her
vocation to save her sister, though she die in the attempt.

On her return home she tells her Greek tutor, the Fox,
how she has found Psyche alive, though she cannot bring
herself to tell him of the glimpse of the palace. In retrospect, and with the help of the Fox's clear-headed rationalism, she is gradually able to empty the valley of most of
its numinous quality.

On a second visit she tells Psyche that their tutor
believes the princess is being taken advantage of by some
tramp or runaway who pretends in darkness he is a god,
and she begs Psyche to steal a look at her husband in his
sleep. When Psyche refuses to disobey her husband's
wishes (she is sure a god must have some reason), Orual
plunges a dagger through her own arm and promises to kill
both herself and Psyche if she persists in her delusion. She
leaves a lamp with Psyche and camps on the other side of
the river. That night Orual sees a blinding light and in the

midst of a terrible storm hears the most inconsolable weeping she has ever known, a weeping which goes on and on until it fades into the distance. A figure surrounded by dazzling light, a beautiful figure which looks like a man, appears to Orual in the storm and tells her "You also shall be Psyche" (p. 174). She returns to her father's palace in unspeakable sorrow and remorse.

The rest of the book tells the story of Orual's efforts to atone for the jealous and possessive love which made her lose Psyche. She dons a veil which she wears the rest of her life to hide her ugliness. Her father dies, and as the new ruler of Glome she submerges herself in work. She does much for her people, yet before the end of the book she discovers that she is still using others for her own purposes—the head captain of her army, her tutor the Fox, her sister Redival. No one else can have his own life, for she needs them all for her uses, which are always noble and commendable but nevertheless hers.[24]

Her hatred for Ungit, the shapeless stone which is worshipped by her people, increases as she adds to her account against the gods; to her they seem ever

> to hint and hover, to draw near us in dreams and oracles . . . to be dead silent when we question them and then glide back and whisper (words we cannot understand) . . . when we most wish to be free of them; . . . what is all this but cat-and-mouse play. . . . Why must holy places be dark places? (p. 249)

Yet for all her rebellion against the gods, Orual discovers there is a wholesome awe about the House of Ungit, an indispensable something which the Fox's rationalistic philosophy can neither explain nor provide. It is especially interesting to see how Lewis plays off the dark idolatry of Ungit-worship against the best which pagan enlightenment can afford, represented in the Greek culture of the Fox. It becomes clear that Ungit is a fertility goddess (she is called Aphrodite by the new priest—p. 308), and to Orual an

---

[24] The book is written in two parts, the second comprising only fifty pages, which are Orual's attempt to set down, before her last illness kills her, what she has discovered about herself since she wrote her indictment of the gods.

image of the demon within. For near the end of the novel Orual discovers in a dream that in her devouring of others she is Ungit. Yet Ungit is not wholly evil. Orual is told that all are born into her House and can get free of her only through sacrifice. Thus she represents things-as-they-are, the world in travail for redemption. As the Fox explains to Orual in a vision of the Deadlands (the afterlife), the House of Ungit, with its gilded temple girls and smells of pigeon blood, knew nevertheless that there must be sacrifices (p. 295). For without dying there can be no life. The priest of Ungit had earlier answered the Fox's accusation that he deals in idle superstition and contradiction thus:

> I have heard . . . [Greek wisdom] before. . . . It is very subtle. But it brings no rain and grows no corn; sacrifice does both. . . . Holy places are dark places. It is life and strength, not knowledge and words, that we get in them. Holy wisdom is not clear and thin like water, but thick and dark like blood. (p. 50)

Against all this stands the Fox, who lives his life in accordance with reason and the humane tradition. He is kind, noble, and well disciplined. Yet he is filled with inconsistencies which belie the existence of the great seamless robe which he calls Nature, a thing harmonious and beautiful. He stands for what is "clear, hard, limited, and simple" (p. 303), and yet the world is none of these things. He always has an explanation, yet he trembles before the mysteries of evil and death.

Good and evil merge in each of the characters in this story. Orual is a woman of great strength and integrity, but she discovers what havoc "a vocation, or even a faith, works on human life" (foreword). Ungit is darkness, and yet it is a darkness necessary for the proper reverence before life's mysteries. The Fox is as blind as Orual to the existence of Psyche's god and palace, but he sees many things far more clearly than anyone else, and at the end Lewis makes him Orual's guide through the Deadlands. And even Psyche, who seems innately good and noble, is the one who causes the most sorrow, for her allegiance is to the god of the Mountain.

In the foreword Lewis briefly describes his themes: "the

mind of an ugly woman, dark idolatry and pale enlightenment at war with each other and with vision, and the
havoc which a vocation, or even a faith, works on human
life." The latter might apply as well to Psyche as to Orual.
There is no undue pride in her dedication, yet simply by
loving the god of the Mountain she must suffer and cause
suffering. Orual writes near the end of her book:

> The Divine Nature wounds and perhaps destroys us merely by
> being what it is. We call it the wrath of the gods; as if the
> cataract in Phars were angry with every fly it sweeps down in its
> green thunder. (p. 284)[25]

In her wrath against the gods Orual wrote her book.
And then when at last she is brought before them in a
vision, she finds that her elaborate arguments, defenses,
and accusations have shrivelled to a very tiny scroll. Before
the court she can speak only what she truly feels and truly
knows. She shouts her complaint over and over again:
"That there should be gods at all, there's our misery and
bitter wrong. . . . We want to be our own" (p. 291). There
is silence in the court and at last the judge says, "Are you
answered?" "Yes," Orual replies, for she knows the complaint gives the answer:

> Lightly men talk of saying what they mean. . . . I saw well why
> the gods do not speak to us openly, nor let us answer. Till that
> word can be dug out of us, why should they hear the babble
> that we think we mean? How can they meet us face to face till
> we have faces? (p. 294)

Then Orual is led by the Fox, who functions in Part II
as a Jungian dream analyst, to examine the walls of the
palace. They are painted with stories which depict four
hard tasks which Psyche has performed in doing penance

---

[25] Cf. Lewis' comment in his introduction to *Arthurian Torso* (London:
Oxford, 1948), pp. 176-177: "Who can seek the Grail without damaging the
Round Table? ('Son, why hast thou thus dealt with us?') The tragic unity of
Man decrees that the sanctification of each should be costly not only to
Christ, not only to his fellow Christians, but, more bewilderingly, to those
whose shattered parental ambition or wounded natural affection reproach him
with dumb pain and total misunderstanding—Son, why hast thou thus dealt
with us?"

for her disobedience of the god of the Mountain. Orual notices with what ease Psyche sorts the giant heaps of seeds, finds golden wool, gets water from the Styx and beauty from Persephone. How, Orual asks, could she do such things and be unscathed? The Fox replies: "Another bore nearly all the anguish" (p. 300). The idea of Substituted Love, found in the works of Charles Williams, supplies the key here. Orual and Psyche are one in a way they could never have been under happy, carefree circumstances. They are one because of what they have borne together and for each other. Thus the god's prophecy, "You also shall be Psyche," has come true. At last they are reunited and when the invisible god of the Mountain comes to bless them, Orual looks in the pool of the pillared court where they stand and she sees two Psyches, "both beautiful (if that mattered now) beyond all imagining, yet not exactly the same" (pp. 307-308).

Till We Have Faces is the most complex and perhaps the most beautiful myth Lewis has ever done. It is not so much of a piece as *Perelandra* or *Out of the Silent Planet.* There are levels of meaning and, in contrast to the others whose themes radiate out from the central story, the development here might be called centripetal because of the way the several themes interlock and move toward the center. That center on which the characterizations of Orual, Psyche, the Fox, and Ungit all finally focus is fittingly described by the title. *Till We Have Faces* is also the most compassionate of Lewis' novels. So tempered are the judgments and so understandingly are the misguided described that it is not easy to tell when the Fox, for example, speaks for Lewis and when Lewis is making him a satirical figure. The novel communicates a sense both of awe and of longing which some will find more convincing than in his earlier works.

This story has several important Jungian features. It is told by the *animus* (personification of the male counterpart of a female character) of Orual. It plays upon the conflicts between thinking and feeling which so interested Jung. It employs dreams to facilitate self-understanding. It recognizes the powerful depths of the *psyche* and uses such archetypes as the plague which demands sacrifice, the innocent atoner, the prideful ruler, the jealous sister, the expiation through tasks, and the journey to the under-world. It uses the Jungian term *psyche* as the name for one of the main characters and, in keeping with Jung's Eastern tendencies, the name Psyche gives to Orual, "Maia," means in Hindu thought the illusion that denies the reality. And Orual moves steadily toward individuation (the Jungian goal of consciousness) through suffering and increased understanding.

I find *Till We Have Faces* the most difficult of all Lewis' works to write about, for when my analysis is done, there are aspects left over which do not fit in with any systematic approach. In this his last work of fiction Lewis clearly acknowledges the limits of reason and the corrupting effects of self-will, operating even in the name of reason and virtue. It seems to be a confessional novel in which he who had been so impatient and hard on certain attitudes reaches a place of withholding judgment for the sake of charity.

Till We Have Faces is remarkable on one other count. It contains the only instance of Lewis' identifying *Sehnsucht* with a person. Psyche longs for the god of the Mountain, but she also is identified with the beauty of goodness in such a way that she inspires longing in others. And the way in which this longing is purified and enables Orual indeed to become herself is the burden of the story.

Sehnsucht *and the emptying of the universe*

The casual reader of Lewis' poetry and fiction is bound to wonder why all this preoccupation with never-never lands, awesome spirits, dryads, centaurs, and the like. It is possible that Lewis pushes some of these things rather far for the capacities of most modern readers. But it must be pointed out that his handling of the Romantic's stock in trade is something exceedingly special. There is no super-ficial, escapist art here. Romantic materials in Lewis' hands turn out always to have cosmic implications, and his delib-erate use of much that seems outmoded is intended to reflect values which our age has lost. The villain in the process of emptying the universe of dryads, centaurs, etc., is of course the scientist. Yet Lewis' quarrel is not with the scientific method. It is with the bogus priests of technology and progress who would apply science to all of life in such a way that the spirit dwindles or is channelled into an evangelistic, well-planned secularism.

In *Spirits in Bondage*, Lewis shows his early awareness of how spiritual and material realities co-inhere:

> We need no barbarous words nor solemn spell
> To raise the unknown. It lies before our feet;
> There have been men who sank down into Hell
>   In some suburban street.
>
> And some there are that in their daily walks
> Have met angels fresh from sight of God,
> Or watched how in their beans and cabbage-stalks
>   Long files of faerie trod.[26]

Other poems in the same collection, especially "The Star Bath" and "How He Saw Angus the God," voice a similar theme but lay no blame on any movement or philosophy. A later poem, "Conversation Piece: The Magician and the Dryad," analyzes the problem further. Here the magician, whom I take to represent the scientist, releases the nymph from her tree:

> . . . She vanishes. And now
> The tree grows barer every moment.
> The leaves fall. A killing air
> Sighing from the Country of Men
> Has withered it.
> The tree will die.[27]

The magician-scientist is amoral, as Merlin in *That Hideous Strength* is amoral. But men can use his powers for

26 " 'Our Daily Bread,' " *Spirits in Bondage*, pp. 86-87.

27 "Conversation Piece: The Magician and the Dryad," *Punch*, 217 (July 20, 1949), 71.

118

good or ill.[28]   In the interplanetary trilogy most of the
villains are scientists, but their sin lies not in their method
but in trying to use that method out of its proper place.
There are scientists among the *séroni* in the Utopian society of Malacandra, yet for them all their devices are means,
not ends, and their method is limited to exploring the
physical world. They make no incursions into the realm of
the spiritual, and they make no cult out of Progress and
the Life-Force, etc.

Lewis believed that the scientific approach, because it is
usually oriented in a Naturalistic view of the world, can be
used to rob certain human experiences (particularly *Sehnsucht* and the sense of the numinous) of their real significance. A cogent discussion of this problem is found in a
preface he wrote for a book which continues to attract an
enthusiastic minority of readers. *The Hierarchy of Heaven
and Earth: A New Diagram of Man in the Universe* was
written by D. E. Harding and published in 1952. In his
preface Lewis says that he does not wholly agree with
Harding's arguments but believes the book should be read
because it is an "attempt to reverse a movement of
thought which has been going on since the beginning of
philosophy." This movement shows a rough one-way
progression in the process whereby man has come to know
the universe:

> At the outset the universe appears packed with will, intelligence,
> life, and positive qualities; every tree is a nymph and every
> planet a god. . . . The advance of knowledge gradually empties
> this rich and genial universe: first of its gods, then of its colours,
> smells, sounds, and tastes, finally of solidity itself as solidity was
> originally imagined. (p. 9)

As man, by inductive thinking and eventually by the
scientific method, removes these things from the world
"they are transferred to the subjective side of the account:
classified as our sensations, thoughts, images, or emo-

[28] It is interesting in this connection to observe that the warning voiced
against scientism in *Out of the Silent Planet* was written almost a decade
before Hiroshima excited a chorus of protest that the human mind had
outstripped the spirit.

tions." Subjective reality is continually enlarged at the expense of Objective reality and the same method "now proceeds to empty ourselves."

> Just as the Dryad is a "ghost," an abbreviated symbol for all the facts we know about the tree foolishly mistaken for a mysterious entity over and above the facts, so the man's "mind" or "consciousness" is an abbreviated symbol for certain verifiable behavior: a symbol mistaken for a thing. (p. 9)

Lewis goes on to attack the theory of Max Müller that mythology is a disease of language. This theory, he says, is a consequence of having transferred too much to the Subjective side of the account:

> For we are given to understand that . . . all our previous theologies, metaphysics, and psychologies were a by-product of our bad grammar. . . . All the questions which humanity has hitherto asked with deepest concern for the answer turn out to be unanswerable, not because the answers are hidden from us . . . but because they are nonsense questions like "How far is it from London Bridge to Christmas Day?" (p. 10)

The end result of the process is that man in emptying the universe of the gods has emptied himself not only of dignity but also of rationality:

> While we were reducing the world to almost nothing we deceived ourselves with the fancy that all its lost qualities were being kept safe (if in a somewhat humbled condition) as "things in our own mind." Apparently we have no mind of the sort required. The Subject is as empty as the Object. Almost nobody has been making linguistic mistakes about almost nothing. By and large, this is the only thing that has ever happened. (p. 11)

This doctrine, while generally rather unpalatable, has its comforts, especially for the leaders of totalitarian states. It is easier to torture, brainwash, and execute if one has such convictions, for according to this view, a man "has no 'inside' except the sort you can find by cutting him open" (p. 11).

Lewis blames Hume for accelerating this process of emptying the Object. Yet in justice to the Scotsman, Lewis notes wryly, he did warn us not to try to keep our minds in the shape this philosophy requires; "he recommended backgammon instead" (p. 11). For, logically, "backgammon" is the only escape from the ridiculousness of it all—unless there is some possibility of seeing the Objective account in a different way. It is this which Harding's book tries to do, at times with brilliant illustration and persuasiveness but too esoterically for the current temper in philosophy. Lewis himself, standing somewhat aloof from Harding's arguments (though he is glad for any reasonable attempt in this direction), admits there is no possibility of returning to animism. "No one supposes that the beliefs of prehistoric humanity, just as they stood before they were criticized, can or should be restored" (p. 12). But, he asks, has there not been some rash concession in the radical empiricism which has brought us to absurdity?

Sehnsucht and numinous awe—related to one another in their basic awareness of disorientation—either belong to the purely Subjective side of the account or they have some relation to Objective reality. Is it maladjustment to physical environment which causes man to experience awesome mystery and what Henry Vaughan called "bright shootes of everlastingnesse"? What are the causes of the disorientation? These questions turn us to a consideration of what Lewis regards as the "rash concession" of radical empiricism and to a conclusion of the ontological quest which is stimulated by longing.

VI THE LOCATION OF JOY

Schill: My life has passed by like a stupid dream. I've hardly once been out of this town. A trip to a lake a year ago. It rained all the time. And once five days in Berlin. That's all.

Claire: The world is much the same everywhere.

—Dürrenmatt, *The Visit*

From a toy garden of moss to Norse mythology, from tales of dressed animals to music, gardens, and valleys which awaken severe delight—a delight which often seems totally incommensurate with the immediate cause. What does it signify? This is a question to which C. S. Lewis addresses himself in much of his poetry, fiction, and criticism. He is not content to set forth in story and verse that elusive experience he calls Joy. As a don he must go on to ask: whence and why?

A number of explanations have gained acceptance both among psychologists and among literary men. E. M. W. Tillyard says in *Poetry: Direct and Oblique* that behind "Primal Joy-Melancholy" lies the growth of man's self-consciousness and his gradual ascent over the other animals. Accepting the burdens of self-consciousness brings Melancholy and a desire for the lost spontaneity and carefree bliss of the animals. The Joy is tied up also with man's ability to foresee progress and to enjoy the future (pp. 50-51). Thus the explanation is to be seen in the light of the Jungian theory of racial memory.

Another explanation, advanced by Sir Harold Nicolson, leans heavily on Behavioral psychology. In *Journey to Java* he explores the biographies of men like Baudelaire, Byron, and Kierkegaard, who were plagued by apparently causeless melancholy. (Melancholy in the sense of depression is of course not the same as *Sehnsucht,* but that mysterious sadness which strikes suddenly and seemingly without any immediate motivation is like the piercing nostalgia Lewis calls *Sehnsucht.* And those who suffer from such melancholy often have moments of apparently causeless joy— e. g., Goethe, Rousseau.) Nicolson comes to the conclusion that most men who suffer "causeless" melancholy "have been cursed either with some deformity which hampers biological fulfillment, or with some functional weakness which prevents the easy elimination of waste products." (Sainte-Beuve had hypospadias, Lucretius was impotent, Nietzsche and Verlaine had underdeveloped pituitary glands.)[1]

A third explanation is to be found in the wish-fulfillment theory set forth by Freud. Joy (in Lewis' special sense) is explained as compensation for unhappy circumstances. At its most intense (when it verges on mystical experience), it wells up out of that uncontrolled reservoir of energy and desire, the Id. It thus represents a strenuous affirmation of the life-force—often in the midst of untoward circumstances.[2] In Koestler's *Darkness at Noon,* for example, Rubashov experiences the "oceanic sense" as he faces execution.

Lewis accepts none of these explanations as anywhere near complete. He is friendlier toward Jung than toward Freud, for he believes that the former provides a "much more civil and humane interpretation of myth and

[1] *Journey to Java*, pp. 233-234.

[2] Sigmund Freud, *The Future of an Illusion* (London: Hogarth, 1928), especially chapter four. Writers influenced by Freudian and Bergsonian thought have made much of this theory. For example, Shaw's preface to *St. Joan* explains Joan's visions as being the result of "that pressure upon her of the driving force which is behind evolution"—(New York: Brentano's, 1924), p. xxii.

imagery."[3] But he criticizes Jung for seeming to say that the reenacting of prehistoric behavior is in itself exciting and impressive. "We reproduce very ancient modes of behavior in all our humblest animal operations—when we scratch [for example]. . . ." Lewis believes the mystery of primordial images is far deeper than mere time. John D. Haigh points out that Lewis would not accept Jung's view of "transcendent intuitions . . . as projections, that is, as psychic contents that were extrapolated in metaphysical space and hypostasized," Lewis regards them, according to Haigh, as broken and imperfect fragments of divine revelation, and resists any attempt to reduce numinous experience to purely human terms. "As regards the archetypes, Lewis, unlike Jung, is a Realist (in the medieval sense) and a Platonist."[4]

Yet Lewis is grateful to psychoanalysis for offering some kind of depth after Materialism had seemed to rob so many experiences of any validity beyond the neurological. And precisely this would be his objection to Nicolson's explanation. A good many things can be explained by Behavioral psychology if one starts with the assumption that certain experiences (e. g., reverential fear in the presence of the numinous) deal with delusions.[5] In *The Personal Heresy* Lewis says that numerous critics of literature have come to accept (half-heartedly perhaps) the picture of the universe which popularized science gives them: "everything except the buzzing electrons is subjective fancy." In so doing the critic assumes that "all poetry must come out of the poet's head and express . . . his pure, uncontaminated . . . 'personality' [hypospadias and all], because outside the poet's head there is nothing but the interplay of blind forces." But, Lewis says, he forgets that

[3] C. S. Lewis, "Psycho-analysis and Literary Criticism," *Essays and Studies by Members of the English Association*, 27 (1941), 7-21. Lewis drew on Jungian theory in a poem called "A Footnote to Pre-history," *Punch*, 217 (Sept. 14, 1949), 304. For a perceptive study of Jung, see June Singer, *Boundaries of the Soul: The Practice of Jung's Psychology* (Garden City, N.Y.: Anchor Press, 1973).

[4] John D. Haigh, *The Fiction of C. S. Lewis*, University of Leeds doctoral dissertation, 1962.

[5] *Out of the Silent Planet*, p. 151.

"if Materialism is true, there is nothing else inside the poet's head either." For a consistent Materialism must see the universe and all men as the undesigned "results of impersonal and irrational causes" (pp. 28-29).

A more formidable explanation is presented in another theory of Freud's, closely related to his explanation of the "oceanic sense." It is the theory most often associated with his name, i. e., that most human activities derive their motive power from the libido. This would make of *Sehnsucht* a symbolic representation of the "fore-pleasure" of copulation. Anticipation is fully as important as fulfillment, and after fulfillment is experienced there may arise a not unpleasant sadness, similar to what the quester feels when he reaches the Garden of Hesperides or the Well at the World's End. The relationship between *Sehnsucht* and the libido is not to be dismissed easily. Lewis believes there is a genuine, though often exaggerated, connection here.

Sex and Sehnsucht

In "Psycho-analysis and Literary Criticism" Lewis attacks Freudian theories of art. In *Mere Christianity* he calls the great psychologist a rank amateur in philosophy,[6] and attempts to show how Freud's insights, while brilliant and often valid, end in making all aesthetic activities a mere by-product of sex. Lewis does not doubt that some works of art have begun as wish-fulfillment dreams (e. g., the novels of Charlotte Brontë). But he objects to the Freudian habit of ending the explanation here, interpreting characters, plot, etc., in sexual terms. He questions in particular the reading of various poetic images as mere disguises for parts of the body:

> If in the **Romance of the Rose** the erotic thought owes much of its poetical charm to the garden, why should the garden in **Paradise Lost** owe all its poetical charm to the erotic world? . . . A necklace of pearls is put round a woman's neck because we think pearls beautiful. If we thought nothing but woman beauti-

[6] New York: Macmillan, 1952, p. 69.

ful we could not beautify women—we should have no materials
with which to do so.[7]

In other words, humanity must be interested in many
other things besides sex. Lewis further argues that the
Freudian critic's attempt to explain so many things in
terms of libidinous symbols often leads the reader to a
feeling of bathos, anti-climax. If, for example, the image of
a garden is only a disguise for the female body, and if the
reader's delight in Book IV of *Paradise Lost* is really erotic,
then "when the psycho-analyst has kindly removed the veil
and conducted me to the thought which (on his view) I
was wanting to think all along," why shouldn't "the affec-
tive temperature" rise, not fall? Why should the most
liberal reader feel that the explanation does something less
than justice to his true feelings when he read the passage—
is he such a prude that everything sexual must be masked?[8]

The Freudian does of course explain this habit of dis-
guising the sexual as a manifestation of inhibition, an
explanation which seems more plausible for nineteenth-
century culture than for our "liberated" age. But laying
aside the question of Freudianism as a gigantic form of
prudery, what, Lewis asks, does the Freudian critic do
with those imaginative experiences which seem to have
little to do with the self, "the unpredictable ecstasy, the
apparent 'otherness' and externality, of disinterested imagination"?[9] He tells of experiencing this unpredictable ecstasy in his childhood in visions of a Snug Town filled with
dressed mice, an imaginative world of which he was not a
part at all. How, he asks, can this sort of imagining be
wish-fulfillment and what can it have to do with sex?

In *Surprised by Joy* he elaborates the point further.
"Those who think that if adolescents were all provided
with suitable mistresses we should soon hear no more of
'immortal longings' are certainly wrong." He learned this
to be a mistake, he says, by the process of repeatedly
making the mistake.

[7] "Psycho-analysis and Literary Criticism," pp. 16-17.
[8] *Ibid.*, p. 14.
[9] *Ibid.*, p. 9.

> I did not recoil from the erotic conclusion with chaste horror.
> . . . My feelings could rather have been expressed in the words,
> "Quite. I see. But haven't we wandered from the real point?"
> Joy is not a substitute for sex; sex is very often a substitute for
> Joy. (p. 170)

Lewis believes, however, that sex can have a spiritual validity which might at times connect it with Joy. In *That Hideous Strength* Mark Studdock discovers that love is, as Plato said, the son of Want, that his desire for Jane—powerful though it is—is nonetheless part of a deeper, unspeakable desire (pp. 430-431, 456-458). When sex is seen in a religious dimension, the role of both husband and wife becomes clearer; the quaint-sounding words, "Husbands, love your wives as Christ has loved the Church" and "Wives, submit yourselves," take on new meaning. Mark learns that there must be gentleness and forbearance. Jane discovers that although the feminist movement would make of any submission to the male a shameful thing, it is nevertheless "an erotic necessity."[10] As God gives true identity when He possesses, so the husband gives to the wife her fullest identity as a woman when she is possessed. And there may be in the experience a quality of adoration not unlike Joy.

This is not to purge sexual desire of its darker passions. Ransom warns the couple against that daintiness in love which would intellectualize the bodily instincts away.[11] (Cf. Williams' comment in *Arthurian Torso*, pp. 58-59: "The maxim for any love affair is 'Play and pray; but on the whole do not pray when you are playing and do not play when you are praying.' We cannot yet manage such simultaneities, and it is difficult for us to believe the early Middle Ages could.") One is also reminded of the sterile cleanliness of the N. I. C. E. headquarters which make man something less than human.[12] As Clinton Trowbridge has

[10] The phrase is from an article entitled "Equality," which Lewis wrote for *The Spectator*, 171 (Aug. 27, 1943), 192. It is instructive to compare this article with Jane Studdock's thinking toward the end of *That Hideous Strength*.

[11] *That Hideous Strength*, p. 321.

[12] *Ibid.*, p. 197.

commented in *The Twentieth Century British Super-natural Novel,* St. Anne's is a place of fecundity, a place of "healthy sexuality."[13] And it can be so because God is there. Thus the Great Dance Lewis describes in the beatific vision which closes *The Problem of Pain* is not, in his thought, a reflection of the erotic interest of the dance. No, the indebtedness, if there is any, lies the other way round. The erotic fulfillment of a good marriage is a foretaste of something yet to be.[14]

It is a sure sign of Lewis' respect for sexuality that he believes sex in the Resurrection will not be atrophied but will be transposed into trans sexuality, a mode of being which will include all that has been good in earthly sexuality and more. He sees the sensuous life being raised from death to exist within the soul. For as God is not in space but space is in God, so sensuous life will be in the soul and richer than ever before (see *Miracles,* especially ch. 14).

Sehnsucht *and Romantic art*

Lewis sees Joy as bearing the same ambivalent relation to art as it bears toward sex. Joy is in it but not to be identified or explained wholly in its terms—sexual or aesthetic. Although it is often through such things as music or painting that Joy is conveyed, art still has its own autonomy which is quite apart from the mystical experience Lewis calls Joy.

Throughout his writings Lewis expresses his conviction that art can speak truth or falsehood, can serve God or the demonic. In *The Great Divorce* the spirit of George Macdonald tells one of the heavenly visitors:

> Ink and catgut and paint were necessary down there, but they are also dangerous stimulants. Every poet and musician and

[13] Unpublished dissertation, University of Florida, 1958. There are passages in Lewis' writing which have the same "pervasive eroticism," the same "glowing, pungent, aromatic quality" which Lewis finds in Williams' Arthurian poems (*Arthurian Torso,* p. 199). The epithalamium at the end of *That Hideous Strength* is a good example.

[14] I have drawn together Lewis' ideas on marriage from various works, especially *The Four Loves,* in an essay called "C. S. Lewis on Eros as a Means of Grace" in *Imagination and the Spirit,* edited by Charles A. Huttar.

artist, but for Grace, is drawn away from the love of the thing he tells, to the love of the telling till, down in Deep Hell, they cannot be interested in God at all but only in what they say about Him. For it doesn't stop at being interested in paint, you know. They sink lower—become interested in their own person-alities and then in nothing but their own reputations. (p. 79)

The spirit also explains that to make a false religion of art is a greater evil than to make a false religion of lust, because the higher something is in the natural order, the more demonic it can become. "It's not out of bad mice or bad fleas you make demons, but out of bad arch-angels" (pp. 97-99).

In the land of Narnia, beauty—even the beauty of music and poetry—can be used against God. The witch in *The Silver Chair* weaves her spell by means of soul-ravishing music.[15] In *The Voyage of the "Dawn Treader"* the three sleepers, covered by their overgrown hair and beards, sym-bolize a decadent art which has lost contact with life and drugged itself with the petals of the lotus (ch. 13). But Lewis has no Puritan fear of art as deception and frivolity. In *Prince Caspian* Lucy and Susan see a wild dance per-formed by centaurs, dryads, satyrs, and other fabled crea-tures, including Bacchus. Yet because Aslan, the great golden-maned lion who is Lewis' symbol for Christ in the Narnia books, is in the dance, it is good.[16] Lewis' position here is clearly summarized by one of the Bright Spirits in *The Great Divorce:* "No natural feelings are high or low, holy or unholy in themselves. They are all holy when God's hand is on the rein. They all go bad when they set up on their own and make themselves into false gods" (p. 93).

Lewis has most carefully elaborated his convictions on the relationship between Romantic art and the Christian faith in his *Arthurian Torso,* a brilliant commentary on Charles Williams' unfinished Arthurian poems. He explains that in these poems, Broceliande (the enchanted sea-wood) represents Romanticism, and Carbonek (where the Grail is kept) represents the place of Grace. Williams made Car-

15 New York: Macmillan, 1953, ch. 12.
16 New York: Macmillan, 1951, ch. 11.

bonek "beyond a certain part of Broceliande," whose enchantments do not have the same effect on all. As Lewis says in his commentary:

> The good man who goes there, by way of unchastened romantic love or what he would call "nature mysticism," will be in danger of perdition. But the bad man who goes there by "thinking with his blood" or worshipping instinct or dabbling in the occult, may be in danger of salvation. . . . This is a hard doctrine for rigid men and a dangerous doctrine for soft men. (pp. 172-173)

Lewis goes on to mention briefly his own indebtedness to Broceliande, the sea-wood. The reader will remember that it was partly through Romanticism that he became interested in Christianity. But, he adds, because ecstatic vision and ineffable beauty can give rise to such great good, they can also be used for great evil. Indeed the Counter-Romantics are right when they attack the "*ersatz* religion*" (Eliot's term) some would make of Romanticism.

Lewis' long-standing quarrel with the Counter-Romantics (it goes back to 1933 when *The Pilgrim's Regress* first appeared) must be understood in the light of this carefully qualified praise for Romantic art. Lewis stands against T. S. Eliot, in particular, in this quarrel. In one of the essays which appeared in *Rehabilitations* Lewis challenges Eliot's low estimate of Shelley, and in *The Personal Heresy* he makes a brief reference to Eliot's snobbery: "For love . . . we must go where it can be found . . . —even to the 'land of lobelias' and tennis flannels" (p. 69). Also, in a poem published in *Punch*, Lewis, writing under the pseudonym "N. W.", remarks about himself that he is so coarse that " . . . things the poets see are obstinately invisible to me. / For twenty years I've stared my level best / To see if evening—any evening—would suggest / A patient etherized upon a table / In vain. I simply wasn't able."[17]

In *The Regress* John meets three pale men from the North (which throughout the book represents the way of reason and system). They are Mr. Humanist, Mr. Neo-

17 "Spartan Nactus," *Punch*, 227 (Dec. 1, 1954), 685.

Angular, and Mr. Neo-Classical (thin disguises for aspects of Irving Babbitt, Eliot, and perhaps T. E. Hulme). They were brought up by Sigismund (Freud), attended the university at Eschropolis (the cynical twenties), and though they have serious differences, they are united in their undying hatred of romantic nonsense. John is impressed by them but discovers that there are those who live even farther North: Marxists, Nietzschean mastermen, and "revolutionary sub-men" of the left and the right. These look forward to someday drinking the blood of all the tough-minded men who consider themselves to have faced life with fearless honesty. John asks the Humanists how they will fight the savages. "By intelligence," they reply. "It moves nothing," says John. "You see the Savage is scalding hot and you are cold. You must get heat to rival his heat. Do you think you can rout a million armed dwarfs by being 'not romantic'?"(p. 109).

Much of the work of the earlier Eliot is alien to Lewis because of its negativism. In fact, there is a rejection of the senses and of creation itself in Eliot which Lewis would challenge—a view of the world more Buddhist than Christian. As he makes clear in *Arthurian Torso,* Lewis held no belief in "a concept of Grace which simply abolishes nature" (p. 175). Even St. John of the Cross "towards the end was encouraged to remember that he liked asparagus" (p. 175). Lewis believed with Williams that man must endure the protests of Nature against Grace. He must not, indeed he cannot, suppress Nature (including the body and the pleasures of the senses) on the grounds that these things are evil. Williams spoke of two Ways: the Affirmation of Images (Romanticism) and the Rejection of Images (Asceticism) (p. 182). Lewis would chide Eliot and other Counter-Romantics for being unnecessarily ascetic.

In contrast to Eliot's tortured misgivings and inability to enjoy, Lewis' writing abounds in the pleasures of the five senses: the scents and colors of Perelandra, the exotic creatures of Narnia, the grim beauty of *Till We Have Faces,* which though laid in a dull, uninteresting land is filled with sensuous detail of a different sort: food, drink, cascading streams, walking in the wind. Screwtape complains in the

Letters that all the real pleasures come from the Enemy:

> He's a hedonist at heart. . . . He makes no secret of it; at His right hand are "pleasures for evermore." . . . He's vulgar, Wormwood. He has a bourgeois mind. There are things for humans to do all day long . . . sleeping, washing, eating, drinking, making love, playing, praying, working. Everything has to be *twisted* before it's any use to us. (p. 112)

There is in the disinterested enjoyment of everyday pleasures "a sort of innocence and humility and self-forgetfulness" which Screwtape does not like (p. 69). To Lewis the "low-brow" pleasures are good if they have these qualities. He does not favor an aristocratic approach to the arts if it means undervaluing the honest enjoyment of story, color, or melody in "low-brow" art. In Lewis' view it is better to enjoy sincerely and disinterestedly (even if the objects of enjoyment are of questionable value as enduring art) than it is to feign an interest in those things which the "best people" are interested in.[18]

But to return to the two Ways. Lewis believes, with Williams, that there is a sense in which the Christian must continually be engaged in both the rejection and the affirmation of images. Of each experience (sex, art, even things ecclesiastical) he must eventually say both "Neither is this Thou" *and* "This is also Thou" (*Arthurian Torso*, p. 151). God is in all His creation, marred though it is by sin, yet finite men must not attempt to identify Him fully with anything in creation. While thinkers like Eliot, Barth, and Maritain have concentrated on the "Neither is this Thou," Lewis has concentrated on the opposite pole of this tension. He deserves much credit for the way he makes this emphasis. Accenting the positive, rejoicing in the good things of creation is rarely successful in our time, when many feel that they do well to muster a faltering "Yea" in

---

[18] See "Lilies that Fester," *Twentieth Century*, 157 (April, 1955), 330-341, and "High and Low Brows" in *Rehabilitations*. The thesis of the latter essay is summed up in the statement: " 'Vulgar' . . . is really a term of moral reproof. It has nothing to do with the distinction of popular and classic" (p. 111).

the face of despair. Again it was Charles Williams who stimulated Lewis' thought here.

In his Arthurian poems Williams speaks of many Houses which tempt the soul to enter—including worship, love, poetry, philosophy. Each House can lead to Byzantium (Heaven) and to the Emperor, but each has an autonomy of its own. "All the different Houses," Lewis says in his commentary, "prove true entries to the Empire only on condition of their remaining themselves." A poetry, for example, "directly and consciously subordinated to the ends of edification usually becomes bad poetry" (p. 166). The artist must genuinely respect creation and in attempting both to respect it and to see it with eyes of faith, he will inevitably become involved with difficulties and failures in a way he would not otherwise. "If you do not effectively enter *any* of the Houses all will seem plain sailing" (p. 170).

Lewis' willingness to be identified with Romantic art, even with its problems and failures, shows, I believe, his recognition of this existential dilemma. The Romantic approach has certain liabilities and is often abused. Yet it is a House straight in front of him and he knows from experience it can lead to the Emperor.

Other things which Joy is not

We have seen that Lewis refuses to equate either sex or Romantic art with *Sehnsucht,* though he recognizes close connections. There remain two other explanations which demand a hearing. One is the idea, best set forth by Wordsworth, that this strange mystical experience so like adoration is a remembering of childhood and infancy. That period of innocence and security, when we were close to Nature and to God, is also celebrated by men like Pater and James Anthony Froude, who remember their childhood homes as heaven upon earth.[19] Lewis regards this

[19] See Walter Pater's "The Child in the House" in *Miscellaneous Studies* (New York: Macmillan, 1900), p. 154, and Froude's *The Nemesis of Faith* (London: Routledge, 1903), p. 18.

approach as basically a re-creation of the past, an attempt to make a golden time for solace and dreaming. (He comments in *Surprised by Joy* that many historians do the same thing with the Renaissance—p. 71.)

Paradoxically, as he notes in his autobiography, this idealization of the past, particularly in Wordsworth, actually expresses the thing whose loss is being lamented. "The very nature of Joy makes nonsense of our common distinction between having and wanting. . . . To have is to want and to want is to have." As a young Romantic, Lewis discovered that the very moment of longing for the sweet pang of Joy was itself such a pang. He is sure that "all that sense of the loss of vanished vision which fills *The Prelude* was itself vision of the same kind" (*Surprised*, p. 71). If Wordsworth could have returned to "those moments in the past, he would not have found the thing itself but only the reminder of it. . . . The books or the music in which we thought the beauty was located will betray us if we trust to them; it was not *in* them, it only came *through* them."[20]

What comes through these things is not a sense of security or peace. This is far from a cozy universe, and it is not settled happiness but fleeting joys that glorify our past. Thus the Joy of which Lewis speaks is more like the momentary effects of a drug. In *Till We Have Faces* Orual says: "I understand why men become drunkards. For the way it worked on me was—not at all that it blotted out . . . sorrows—but that it made them seem glorious and noble, like sad music, and I somehow great and reverend for feeling them" (p. 224).

But out of his own experience Lewis warns against valuing Joy as one would value a drug which could produce a similar effect. Perhaps this is the worst mistake of all. For in his view it would use something profoundly significant to titillate the emotions. Joy, he says, is a by-product:

Its very existence presupposes that you desire not it but something other and outer. If by any perverse askesis or the use of

20 *The Weight of Glory*, pp. 4-5.

any drug it could be produced from within, it would at once be
of no value. For take away the object, and what, after all, would
be left? A whirl of images, a fluttering sensation in the dia-
phragm, a momentary abstraction.[21]

We know from the earlier chapters of this study what
Lewis regards as the object of Joy. To say it is God seems
too easy, for to the Christian everything reflects God in
some way and He is in everything. Lewis is not willing to
make the explanation that simple.

The Pagan vision

One of the main sources of Lewis' appeal is his high regard
for Paganism, for we live in an age which is more Pagan
than Christian. The *pagani* were originally worshippers in
the fields, and today's city dwellers—cut off from nature in
machine-like jobs and in high-rise apartments with windows that do not open—are intent on finding some oneness
with nature.

Lewis regards William Morris as the best and least self-
conscious Pagan who has written in English. He finds in
Morris the "fresh fruit of naive experience, uncontaminated by theorizing" (see his essay on Morris in *Rehabilitations*). This freshness Lewis experienced in both the Northern and Mediterranean myths that so enthralled him as a
boy. He felt that being a Christian does not require a
denial of beauty in those myths, that there are real goods
in Paganism which can indeed be caught up and developed
further in Judaism and Christianity. Those who have no
other revelation of God than that afforded by nature and
human magnanimity will, in Lewis' opinion, be judged
only in terms of what they have been given. In *The Last
Battle* the noble worshipper of a pagan god discovers in a
moment of apocalyptic revelation that all along he has
actually worshipped Aslan the divine lion without knowing
the real name.

As Paganism is the religion of nature, so Paganism is the

---

[21] *Surprised by Joy*, p. 168.

religion of poetry which celebrates created things.[22] To deny what is good in Paganism would be to set aside nature in a way which assumes that we are angels and not men. Angels do not eat or sleep or make love, for they do not live in nature. For Lewis there are no *immediate* experiences of God, for all that we know of God comes through some created thing: language, art, people, history, ritual. God may reveal Himself directly to angels without using the things He has made, but Lewis does not believe He deals in this way with human beings.

Lewis maintains that the *mythos* of the New Testament transposes all the best visions of Paganism into another key of richer harmony—whether they be the transcendent monotheism of Akhenaten, the theistic leap of Plato, or such Pagan Christs as Adonis, Balder, and Osiris. There is a case to be made for the "immediately sub-Christian virtues" (Lewis' term in *Rehabilitations*) of fortitude, integrity, courage, etc., and while the Christian virtues of faith, hope, and charity are higher virtues in that they proceed from a response to God's initiatives in Christ, the Pagan virtues are not to be despised except when they lead to self-congratulation.

In *Miracles* Lewis speaks of the Descent and Re-Ascent involved in the Incarnation and its consequences. This idea sounds very much like Barfield's explanation of evolution as being like a capital "U." There is a downward journey away from Nature, and then through Spirit progressively incarnating itself in the phenomena and in human consciousness, there begins at the point of the Incarnation of Christ a movement upward toward Spirit again, in which it assumes all things to itself.[23] Christ comes among men emptying Himself. Thus, Lewis says, it is not surprising that one often finds greater beauty and allure in the pagan myths than in the Biblical ones. Just as Christ undergoes a *kenosis* as the incarnate God, so the stories closest to the Incarnation are the least glamorous of the Biblical myths:

22 *English Literature in the Sixteenth Century*, p. 342.
23 Owen Barfield, *Romanticism Comes of Age* (Middletown, Conn.: Wesleyan, 1967), pp. 84-85.

birth in a barn, healing lepers, eating broiled fish after His resurrection. The myths themselves have undergone a humiliation compared to ancient Greek and even early Old Testament stories. By their very mundaneness and austerity they point to the self-emptying of the God-Man.

But there is the Re-Ascent of Christ in which He catches up all the best in Buddhist, Hindu, Islamic, and Jewish thought. All things cohere in Him and in these religions there is no valid perception of Godhead which is set aside and no hope or anticipation which will not be fulfilled in Him.

Sehnsucht *and the masks of God*

In a study such as this it seems imperative to face the relevance of the work of Joseph Campbell. Yet this is difficult to do, for there is no evidence that Lewis knew Campbell's theories. There is no record of any book by Campbell being among the 3,000 in Lewis' personal library and he never quotes from him in his books. Among the twentieth-century critics Lewis acknowledges as having contributed to his own critical approaches, he names Wilson Knight, Caroline Spurgeon, Maude Bodkin, and Owen Barfield. He may have absorbed some of Campbell's ideas through one of them, but this is only speculation.

Campbell, so far as I can discover, has never made any direct comment on the *Sehnsucht* archetype, but being heavily influenced by Jung, he would probably see this archetype as a complex of remembered and half-remembered loss. Thus it would point entirely backward in time and have little if any ontological significance. Or following Freud, he might well account for the archetype as an aspect of the "oceanic sense," that awareness of extended being in which the individual, relatively weak and helpless, believes he is part of a very large and comprehensive whole. This sense is usually accompanied by a deep peace and even longing as for some lost unity with nature.

Both Lewis and Tolkien have written of their belief that all people desire communication with the animals. Perhaps some of the interest in bestial sex experience in current literature represents, on a crude level, this primal desire for unity with other forms of life. Certainly the desire to vacation in the wilderness reflects this drive. Yet while *Sehnsucht* includes an awareness of loss, how can we account for the element of severe joy which is also part of it? As Jung observes, a "secret unrest gnaws at the roots of our being" and yet our hearts "glow."[24] Why the glow? It is as if in recognizing our sadness at some unidentifiable loss, we gain a sense of dignity and destiny which would otherwise be denied to us.

But to settle for *Sehnsucht* as being only a compensatory feeling seems not to do justice to its variety and complexity. Lewis, the untiring foe of Reductionism, would never approve such an explanation. If love is only lust, religion only aberrant psychology, thought only cerebral biochemistry, and the universe only a mathematical construct, the world would not be the rich and wild and startling place it manifestly is. So while Lewis would honor Joseph Campbell's work, he would resist any explanation of *Sehnsucht* which becomes nominalist and developmentalist. He would insist that the experience points forward as well as backward and that with this idea, as with other concepts, one must articulate a theory of ideas before he can fit the parts of the puzzle together.

The object of "Joy"

In speaking of *Sehnsucht* in the works of Spenser, Lewis says in *English Literature in the Sixteenth Century* that such longing would not be regarded by a Christian Platonist "as a horrible form of spiritual dram-drinking" (pp. 356-357). Rather it "would logically appear as among the sanest and most fruitful experiences we have," for the object of longing "really exists and really draws us to itself."[25]

In all the various Christian views of the world the concreteness or reality of an experience is not measured by

24 *Psychological Reflections* (New York: Pantheon, 1953), p. 24.
25 *English Literature in the Sixteenth Century*, pp. 356-357.

138

empirical authentication. The Real is often "unseen"—as we usually think of seeing, and although practical considerations demand that we concentrate on the reality of tables, chairs, food, work, etc., we must not (especially in Lewis' view) fall into the trap of thinking these are the most real entities. The *eldila* of Venus tell Ransom: "You have only an appearance, small one. You have never seen more than an appearance of anything—not of Arbol [sun], nor of a stone, nor of your own body."[26] For Lewis and the other Oxford Christians "reality begins not in the seen but the unseen," as Clyde Kilby puts it.

> Anything "merely" this or that is likely to be, in an ultimate sense, deceiving. Abstraction of any sort tends to denigrate the wholeness suggested by intuition and philosophy and to which images and symbols are an important avenue of understanding. Everything is greater than the sum of its parts.[27]

Mark Studdock in *That Hideous Strength* believes that as a thoroughly anti-metaphysical sociologist he has succeeded in separating the real, everyday world from the purely speculative world of ideas and values. But he discovers that he keeps resisting the peculiar things the demonic Frost and Wither want him to do as a test of his obedience and capacity for objectivity. The meaningless exercises and petty obscenities finally force him to discover that something deep within him would like to dispel the whole business with "one good roar of coarse laughter." He had always thought that ideas were "things inside one's own head." But now, when his mind was weary and bewildered, "the idea of the Straight or the Normal" loomed up in front of him, "something which objectively existed quite independently of himself and had hard rock surfaces which would not give" (p. 367). He began to see that all along he had believed "as firmly as any mystic in the superior reality of the things that are not seen" (p. 93), in classes, elements, vocational groups, populations. And

26 *Perelandra*, p. 216.

27 In *Shadows of Imagination*, ed. by Mark Hillegas (Carbondale, Ill.: Southern Illinois U.), pp. 75-76.

here was an idea not of his making, an idea which was stubbornly real.[28] Thus Mark's discovery underscores Lewis' belief that a radical empiricism often falls into the inconsistency (or rash concession) of regarding theological concepts as purely speculative while accepting readily other ideas which have no more foundation in experience.

The idea of God is stubbornly real to Lewis, was real to him long before he wanted it to be (see Chapter II). As J. B. S. Haldane points out, Lewis never attempts to deduce the existence of God from the physical universe.[29] But he makes indirect use of the ontological argument and variations on that argument. In *The Case for Christianity* he argues that the majority of men recognize the existence of moral obligation; in *The Problem of Pain* he shows how this moral sense together with the sense of the numinous causes men to be uneasy before the idea of divine goodness; and throughout his fiction and poetry he tells how all the desires of men seem to lead to "false Florimels."[30] (When Prince Caspian of Narnia reproves Edmund for having lived in a round world and never having told him about it, Edmund says: "There's nothing particularly exciting about a round world once you're there.")[31]

The ontological argument, as Lewis uses it, is summarized in the preface to *The Pilgrim's Regress:* "If a man deliberately followed this desire [*Sehnsucht*], pursuing the false objects until their falsity appeared and then resolutely abandoning them, he must come at last into the clear

---

[28] The idea of the Straight would, in Lewis' view, come to Mark from the "Tao," that authority which operates in the affairs of all men and implements an overarching vision of goodness and truth. Lewis most fully describes this concept in *The Abolition of Man,* which asserts that basic values are unprovable because they are axiomatic, that radically new values cannot be invented because there is something in the nature of things (or in man's nature) which resists going against the Tao. In the light of recent discoveries in sociology and psychology, Lewis perhaps does not allow for enough relativism. But this book is a bracing counterattack on various forms of popular relativism which glibly seek to debunk all value judgments except their own.

[29] "God and Mr. C. S. Lewis," *The Rationalist Annual for Year 1948* (London: Watts, 1949), pp. 78-85.

[30] *The Pilgrim's Regress,* p. 8.

[31] *The Voyage of the "Dawn Treader,"* p. 208.

knowledge that the human soul was made to enjoy some object that is never fully given" (p. 10).

Why is this object never fully given? "God cannot give us peace and happiness apart from himself because it isn't there."[32]

In his *Reflections on the Psalms* Lewis makes some observations on the relations between time and eternity which amplify the statement above. With regard to the perennial theological problems of the apparent determinism and exclusivism of Christianity, Lewis (following Boethius) believes that time is only a kind of porthole on eternity and that it is less real than eternity.[33] Without the impingement of eternity, time would be "mere succession and mutability." But fortunately

> we are so little reconciled to time that we are even astonished at it. "How he's grown!" we exclaim, "How time flies!" as though the universal form of our experience were again and again a novelty. It is as strange as if a fish were repeatedly surprised at the wetness of water. And that would be strange indeed; unless of course the fish were destined to become, one day, a land animal.[34]

Lewis makes clear his belief that a desire for God does support the idea of His existence. It is true, he says, that being hungry does not prove we will have bread: "a man may die of starvation on a raft in the Atlantic. But surely a man's hunger does prove that he comes of a race which

[32] *The Case for Christianity*, p. 42.

[33] See *The Great Divorce*, pp. 128f., where a similar point is made. Throughout this book, and elsewhere, Lewis writes of God as the *most real* being and of Hell as partaking of less reality than Heaven—Hell is a place grey, formless, and infinitely monotonous. Also, Earth by comparison with Heaven is less real. In *The Last Battle* Aslan refers to Earth as "the Shadowlands" (p. 183).

[34] *Reflections on the Psalms* (New York: Harcourt, Brace, 1958), p. 138. Santayana speaks to this same subject, though taking a more resigned view, at the end of *My Host the World*. He talks of "the double conflict, the social opposition and the moral agony, that spirit suffers by being incarnate. . . . [Yet] if it were not incarnate it could not be individual. . . . [Perhaps it is] the fate of all spirit to live in a special body and in a special age, and yet, for its vocation and proper life, to be addressed from that center to all life and all being" (New York: Scribner's, 1953), p. 138.

repairs its body by eating and inhabits a world where eatable substances exist."[35]

The point cannot be made airtight of course. There is usually a good Naturalistic explanation for those experiences which Christians believe come from "above." In "Transposition" Lewis discusses the relations of the physical to the spiritual, pointing out that the internal sensations accompanying an experience of intense aesthetic delight may be indistinguishable from the sensations which accompany a "rough channel crossing." The significance of an experience, he believes, can never be derived from approaching it objectively. Sheer analysis of behavior gets nowhere, for "the brutal man never can by analysis find anything but lust in love; the Flatlander can never find anything but flat shapes in a picture; physiology can never find anything in thought except the twitching of grey matter."[36]

Yet so much of intellectual inquiry is directed at analyzing, at explaining, at "outgrowing" the metaphysical. As Screwtape says in the *Letters*: "Real worldliness is a work of time—assisted, of course, by pride, for we teach them [human beings] to describe the creeping death as good sense or Maturity or Experience." Therefore devils must keep men ever on guard against "the incalculable winds of fantasy and music and poetry—the mere face of a girl, the song of a bird, the sight of a horizon" (p. 144).

In his elaboration of the ontological argument, Lewis moulds perhaps his firmest apologetic for Christianity. I cannot share his faith in rational argument as something which will virtually compel a man, if he is honest, toward God. It seems to me that the ontological argument, like all the arguments for God's existence, must be lived through. But Lewis' exploration of *Sehnsucht* is likely to send into the mind of almost any reader "airs and echoes" of something which demands investigation. A radical empiricism must accept some such theory as that of Freud or Tillyard, but once one grants that there may be things in

---

[35] *The Weight of Glory and Other Addresses*, p. 6.
[36] *Ibid.*, p. 25.

human nature which were not first in the five senses, and that these realities have their origin and motive power in God, one sees the world with different eyes. Morality becomes more than social conditioning and expediency, ideas become valid or invalid by criteria which are "built-in" through God's gift of rationality to man, and art's blissful longings take on cosmic implications. In an age plagued by the historical method and a developmentalist explanation for everything, Lewis' theory is courageous and refreshing. There is novelty in his handling of the data, but the basis of his explanation is not novel. Indeed it is part of a worldview which has a long and honorable tradition.

VII SEHNSUCHT AND THE NEW ROMANTICISM

Worshipping snakes or trees, worshipping devils rather than nothing: crying for life beyond life, for ecstasy not of the flesh.
—T. S. Eliot, *The Rock*

The first chapter of this study promised a survey of a specific attitude as that attitude finds expression and explanation in the works of C. S. Lewis. It is obvious that my treatment of Lewis' explanation of *Sehnsucht* has been, for the most part, highly sympathetic. But a few words of evaluation seem in order.

I have most often referred to the attitude or idea which has been my subject by using the term *Sehnsucht* or Joy. However dissimilar bittersweet nostalgia and piercing stabs of happiness may be, they share a quality of exaltation and often come unexpectedly, without any apparent cause. Also, as described in Chapters I and IV, both *Sehnsucht* and Joy reflect a sense of displacement or disorientation which seems often to unite them in the vocabulary of poetic language—e.g., Tillyard's discussion of "primal Joy-Melancholy." Lewis uses the terms interchangeably. But he need not be held accountable for the inclusion of numinous awe under his concept. That has been my doing, partly because I see in numinous awe a closely related experience (a similar feeling of disorientation caused by a sudden confrontation with something "other and outer") and partly because much of what Lewis says in examining numinous awe is closely bound up with his explanation of *Sehnsucht.*

Lewis' biography, literary theory, and his fiction and poetry all demonstrate how the experience of disorientation common to *Sehnsucht* and numinous awe may be regarded ultimately as a hound of Heaven, relentlessly pursuing man in order that he may discover his true identity and home. All our loves are seen as copies of our love for God; He is drawing us to Himself with "cords of infinite desire."[1] Lewis emphasizes the universality of the experience by often clothing traditional Christian concepts in pagan dress as in *Till We Have Faces*, in the atmosphere of other worlds as in *Perelandra* and *Out of the Silent Planet*, or in the Bartasian technique of the Narnia books, wherein things great and even divine are represented by smaller, humdrum things.[2]

I realize that a very good case might be made for explaining most of Lewis' art in Freudian terms. The sensuous beauty of all these never-never lands could be called wish-fulfillment,[3] the preoccupation with longing could reflect the life of a cloistered academic (and until late in life a bachelor), and the fleeting stabs of nostalgia which he experienced from childhood could be related, in part, to the death of his mother—the sudden loss of support, etc.[4] The Freudian, while under heavy attack these days, is still far from being a straw man and I do not presume to use him so. But I believe that Lewis' objections to converting psychoanalysis into a philosophic worldview or a religion (see Chapter VI) point up quite well the difficul-

[1] *Perelandra,* p. 235.

[2] Lewis expresses his admiration for Du Bartas in an essay called "Hero and Leander," Warton Lecture on English Poetry, British Academy (London: Oxford, 1952), p. 33.

[3] Alistair Cooke made this charge in a review of *Perelandra* called "Mr. Anthony at Oxford," *The New Republic,* 110 (April 24, 1944), 578-580.

[4] The chronology of *Surprised by Joy* belies this, however, as I have pointed out in Chapter II.

ties of using such an explanation. There is, in my judgment, too much significant data left over. The conditions under which certain attitudes to life are implemented (insecurity, longing, religious faith) are not necessarily the same as the efficient causes of those attitudes. Dostoevsky cannot be explained by epilepsy or Nietzsche by syphilis. And *Sehnsucht* cannot be explained simply as the result of disturbances in personal life or as an idea begotten by Plato or Plotinus.

The developmentalist theory of ideas is logically no more airtight than the explanations of Christian theology. For the so-called Platonic view of ideas (which asserts the reality of things unseen as a higher sort of reality) is not limited to Plato and those influenced by him. Animism, which existed centuries before his time, presupposed the existence of spirits or souls distinct from matter—transcendent realities if you will. And in the present century, with Plato out of fashion, German Phenomenology and some of the Existentialists (e.g., philosopher-theologian Paul Tillich) have reflected their belief in a transcendental order. While the so-called Platonic view holds that there is an unseen order or reality *above* the more obvious empirical reality, Tillich and the Phenomenologists look rather down into the depths of reality—questioning, searching, penetrating into existence to the level where reality points beyond itself to its "inner infinity."[5] Whether one says there is an unseen order *above* or *within* empirical reality is of little consequence so far as the existence of transcendentals is concerned. In either case, there is an order which transcends the obvious, empirical one.[6]

5 James Luther Adams, "Tillich's Concept," in Paul Tillich, *The Protestant Era*, translated and with a concluding essay by Adams (Chicago: U. of Chicago, 1948), p. 296.

6 Some interpreters of Plato hold that we "see" *forms*, the conceptual element in reality, as clearly as we perceive any *sensory* quality, that these aspects of experience are inseparable. As Professor Charles McCoy has explained it, the formal aspect of experience points to a more enduring reality but not to a "higher" world which exists in a place separate from the world in

Tillich's method of symbolizing this order is naturally less offensive to an age suspicious of the old two-story structure of reality (Nature and Super-nature) razed by Kant. But in fairness to Plato, we must remember that in positing an order of noumenal reality above the empirical he does not act by divine fiat. Platonic thought, like Phenomenology, begins with the phenomena of experience but ends in positing the existence of realities which cannot be empirically verified. Plato locates these in almost geographical terms,[7] while Phenomenology explains these unseen realities in terms of their fundamental psychological validity. The old realist-nominalist controversy is latent here, but my point is that both schools of thought believe in the existence of realities which cannot be absolutely verified by empirical means. In other words, Tillich and the Phenomenologists are simply stating over again a fundamental truth—the old contrast between appearance and reality—upon which man draws in his unique ability to use symbols. I look upon this as a fundamental condition of existence—whatever terms one uses to explain it—something which man would have seen without Plato, in fact had already seen, in animism, before the rise of Greek philosophy.

I do not mean to suggest by this that the Christian understanding of *Sehnsucht* is thereby vindicated. Presuppositions and "faith principles" are still involved. One reader, no less alert or honest than another, might see *Sehnsucht* in quite different terms. I only go on record that Lewis' theological explanation seems most convincing to me. I must echo what Clinton Trowbridge says of Lewis' work: "His mythopoeic imagination is so rich in invention, so broad in scope, so sensuously perceptive in

---

which we are at any moment of existence. Professor McCoy's view finds support in Robert L. Calhoun's essay, "Plato as Religious Realist," which appeared in *Religious Realism*, edited by D. C. McIntosh (New York: Macmillan, 1931).

[7] This is often the way Platonic thought is described by Aristotelians. I doubt that this view does justice to Plato, particularly as a mythmaker.

descriptive detail that, after we . . . [have read him], we have a difficult time viewing the Cosmos through any but Lewis' eyes."[8]

Having said this, I find that my other conclusions must take the form, first, of what some may regard as a devastating admission; second, of noting some important correspondences between Lewis' theory and the conversation which is now going on among some thoughtful people; and third, of a serious claim with regard to the survival of Romanticism in our time.

Lewis' theory as a death-blow to Romanticism

After pursuing this study to the end, I began to see a strange paradox emerging. Lewis' explanation could mean the death of Romanticism, for once the Romantic Way is viewed as one of the roads to Byzantium (and often a long way round), the traveller must inevitably ask himself: Why not take the direct route of Christian mysticism? Lewis himself is aware of this paradox. He says at the end of *Surprised by Joy* that since his conversion he has become less interested in Joy:

> When we are lost in the woods the sight of a signpost is a great matter. He who first sees it cries "Look!" The whole party gathers round and stares. But when we have found the road and are passing signposts every few miles, we shall not stop and stare. They will encourage us and we shall be grateful for the authority which set them up. But we shall not stop . . . though their pillars are of silver and their lettering of gold. (p. 238)

But as Lewis says in *Arthurian Torso*, each of the Houses (poetry, philosophy, love, etc.) which may lead eventually to the Emperor can do so only on the condition that it preserves its own autonomy. One cannot simply *use* Creation; we are too much a part of it. This is the difficult task: to know that Romantic art is often a reflection of man's longing for God and yet still to respect and cherish

8 *The Twentieth Century British Supernatural Novel*, p. 365.

it as art.[9] One can hardly go further than Charles Williams' "Neither is this Thou" and "This also is Thou."

Lewis' willingness to face a profound paradox here is further evidence that far from being a hidebound rationalist, he is able to honor reason, to use the most astringent logic, and yet also to recognize that there are truths which reason cannot ferret out. A narrow rationalism can never be comfortable with paradoxes. But here Lewis has admitted a very great paradox, precisely because he knows that reality in its wholeness does not require arbitrary dichotomies. Thus his concept of *Sehnsucht* can destroy Romanticism only for those who have enthroned it as God. Its proper validity as a way remains. The great difficulty of course is that of effectively entering one of the Houses and yet not mistaking it for Byzantium.[10]

How Lewis' concept meets recent theology and aesthetics

Lewis' understanding of *Sehnsucht*, indebted as it is to medieval tradition, especially Augustine, will naturally find support among contemporary writers who are similarly indebted—e.g., Jacques Maritain, especially in what he says of the Beatific Vision.[11] The concept is also consistent with much that has been written by literary people influenced by Coleridge. Early in the century A. C. Bradley stated well the Coleridgean attitude toward art:

> About the best poetry, and not only the best, there floats an atmosphere of infinite suggestion. The poet speaks to us of one thing, but in this one thing there seems to lurk the secret of all. He said what he meant, but his meaning seems to beckon away

[9] But there is comfort in the paradox. As Lewis explains in "Christianity and Literature" (an essay in *Rehabilitations*), the Christian does not have to elevate art into a religion. His values are not dependent upon aesthetics and he is freed from the oversolemnity and messianic impulses which beset some literary criticism today. This essay is also found in *Christian Reflections* (Grand Rapids: Eerdmans, 1967).

[10] See Chapter VI, p. 132 above.

[11] See *The Degrees of Knowledge* (New York: Scribner's, 1938), especially pp. 8-9, and *Art and Scholasticism* (New York: Scribner's, 1942), especially pp. 45-46, 95-96.

beyond itself, or rather into something boundless which is only focused in it; something also which, we feel, would satisfy not only the imagination, but the whole of us. . . .[12]

Lewis' "Joy" sounds very much like this sense of "all embracing perfection which cannot be expressed in poetic words or words of any kind, nor yet in music or in color, but the suggestion of [which] " still haunts us.[13]

There is also a memorable passage in Alfred North Whitehead describing the restlessness of art. "Great art," he says, "is the arrangement of the environment so as to provide for the soul vivid, but transient, values." It is a necessary condition of art that it be restless: "an epoch gets saturated by the masterpieces of any one style. Something new must be discovered. The human being wanders on." For the soul is seeking "the permanent realization of values extending beyond its former self."[14]

In *Arts and the Man* Irvin Edman says a similar thing: "The arts, in fragments as it were, suggest the goal toward which all experience is moving; . . . those moments of felicity which the fine arts at moments provide . . . [give us] a foretaste of what an ordered world might be."[15]

But the most striking parallel between Lewis' concept and what other contemporary writers have thought is to be found in the work of Paul Tillich. In Tillich's theology God is both immanent and transcendent: He is the ground of being of which this world is a part (this concept being close to Wordsworth's panentheism). Because God is the power of being in which every being participates, His power thus imbues all forms and bursts forth through them, making possible art, science, and all the creative activities of man. The forms of being are filled with an import which man may intuit through experience that is, to some degree at least, "ecstatic."

[12] *Oxford Lectures on Poetry* (London: Macmillan, 1909), p. 26.
[13] *Ibid.,* p. 26.
[14] *Science and the Modern World* (New York: Macmillan, 1926), pp. 290-291.
[15] New York: Norton, 1928, pp. 34-35.

> Ecstasy operates in such a way as to break through the given forms of individual existence, bringing it into union with the ultimate ground of meaning. It is experience of being grasped by the essential power and meaning of reality.[16]

Ecstasy in Tillich's sense does not mean primarily an experience of great emotional upheaval but rather an experience of temporarily transcending oneself. The artist does this when his imagination is acted upon by the "unconditional" (God) and the beholder senses in the aesthetic experience provided through the artist a level of reality otherwise inaccessible. But the beholder does this only as he also is grasped by the unconditional. Thus ecstatic intuition, when it operates in art or wherever, is "the operation of love, the uniting of that which is separated."[17] Though the language is quite different (Tillich tries to avoid traditional theological terms), there are, of course, clear-cut similarities between Tillich's explanation and that of Lewis.

One last parallel, equally striking. In *The Yogi and the Commissar* Arthur Koestler explores the various roads men have laid out for Utopia. He shows that in art, in physics, in politics, many appear to be on a vast pilgrimage. Why? he asks:

> We cannot ask for a common reason, we can only ask for a common denominator in the variety of reasons. . . . Perhaps the common denominator we are looking for can best be described as an "anti-materialistic nostalgia." It is allergic to the rationalism, the shallow optimism, the ruthless logic, the arrogant self-assurance, the Promethean attitude of the nineteenth century; it is attracted by mysticism, romanticism, the irrational ethical values, by mediaeval twilight.[18]

Koestler's "anti-materialistic nostalgia" sounds indeed like a more generalized definition of Lewis' *Sehnsucht*.

There are many other parallels—for example, the vague but violent longing in Sartre and Heidegger, and earlier in

16 James Luther Adams, "Tillich's Concept," in *The Protestant Era*, p. 299.

17 Tillich's words, quoted by Adams, p. 303.

18 New York: Macmillan, 1946, p. 13.

Kierkegaard. But it should be clear by now that Lewis' concept is not alien to the temper of our time. His explanation of the ontological quest of Romanticism comes to a soil prepared to receive it, not only in philosophy and theology but also in literature.

The survival of Romantic art

We are hearing nowadays of a new "ism," Neo-Romanticism. What is it and how is it different from the Romanticism of Wordsworth, Shelley, and Keats?

Once I had begun this study, I was happy to discover that there were others besides myself who did not consider Romanticism either dead or intellectually ridiculous. In 1957 John Bayley's highly provocative book *The Romantic Survival* appeared. He poses this question: Can Romanticism still have "authority and depth as well as excitement and freshness?"—can its visions of the world still "connect swiftly and intimately with the deepest issues of life as does, for example, Wordsworth's vision of the leech-gatherer?"[19]   In seeking an answer, Bayley discusses the work of Yeats, Auden, and Dylan Thomas—poets "who found romanticism at a low ebb . . . but who were able to rediscover its original scope and richness" (pp. 77-78). Bayley believes that Romantic poetry has a special ability to turn whatever it touches into mystery. He shows how the elaborate symbolism and "negative capability" of Yeats achieves this and how the highly unconventional syntax and diction of Thomas is used to the same purpose. Of Thomas' verse he says: It brings the hidden to light, not as explanation, not even as commentary, but as a reality wrested "from the same depths as the experience itself" (p. 198).

This quality of mystery, quintessential to Romanticism, is of a different kind in Auden. In his verse, Bayley says, we see that "Romanticism has anchored itself to the earth once more" (p. 80). The humdrum is far from the

[19] London: Constable, 1957, p. 6.

antithesis of the romantic. Pottering in the garden, whistling, or even mowing the grass is in some way illuminated, invested with a kind of wonder. In contrast to Yeats and Thomas, Auden's poetry does not often reflect the mystic exultation found in Wordsworth or Keats. But much of his work does show a vivid sense of the numinous (especially *The Age of Anxiety*), and some of it has touches of the homely (though here carefully restrained) nostalgia one associates with Romanticism. For example, the mood of longing which pervades his *Christmas Oratorio*[20] is sober and controlled, yet it is longing still. Auden can sketch in a few words a picture of desolation which is strangely gratifying; in 1930 he wrote:

> On the sopping esplanade or from our dingy lodgings we
> Stare out dully at the rain which falls for miles into the
> sea.[21]

As Bayley says of this poem, "everything is hopeless and the country is going to the dogs, but to think this, while staring out at the rain, is somehow no inconsiderable pleasure."[22]

I dwell briefly on Auden because of the three poets Bayley discusses he was the one least likely to be thought of as a Romantic. He usually wrote with an eye on the critics and he was well aware that whatever has survived of Romanticism in our time must be a highly chastened Romanticism.

When C. S. Lewis wrote his preface for the revised edition of *The Pilgrim's Regress*, he also recognized this fact. Echoing words of T. E. Hulme, he admitted that Romanticism is "spilt religion."[23] Hulme as well as Eliot had called for a theological attack on the Romantic *Weltanschauung*. Man is very much a finite creature, they argued. Therefore the poet must not be expected to func-

---

[20] See especially "The Vision of the Shepherds," "At the Manger," and "The Meditation of Simeon" in *For the Time Being: A Christmas Oratorio*.

[21] *Poems*, 1930, No. 22 (quoted by Bayley, p. 130).

[22] *The Romantic Survival*, p. 130.

[23] T. E. Hulme, "Romanticism and Classicism," in *Speculations* (New York: Harcourt, Brace, 1924), p. 118.

tion as a "reservoir full of possibilities."[24] Eliot con-
demned the Yeatsian emphasis on that pregnant uncer-
tainty which would make of poetry "a superhuman mir-
ror-resembling dream."[25] The poet, Eliot answered, is a
man who lives in a real world where he must commit
himself.

On this point Lewis agrees with the Counter-Romantics.
He has repeatedly shown his distrust of that movement
(Bayley traces it back to Keats) which would "dispossess
the Romantic Imagination,"[26] divorcing it from philosophy and theology and confining it to the world of sensation. Eliot believes that a poet, to be of real importance,
should be "committed to a view of things which the reader
can accept or at least respect."[27] Lewis would perhaps not
go that far, but he has said that a poem whose "intellectual
basis is silly, shallow, perverse, or illiberal, or even radically
erroneous, is in some degree crippled by that fact."[28]

In his essay "Criticism in a Mass Society," Auden describes well the presuppositional chasm which divides the
old Romanticism from the new:

> The statement, "Man is a fallen creature, with a natural bias to
> do evil," and the statement, "Men are good by nature and made
> bad by society," are both presuppositions. . . . If, as I do, you
> assent to the first, your art and politics will be very different
> from what they will be if you assent, like Rousseau or Whitman,
> to the second.[29]

Thus, there have been two general ways of modifying
the old Romanticism: either the writer humbles his aspirations in the light of man's fallen state, or he attempts to
separate art from moral considerations, keeping it a thing
apart—beauty for beauty's sake.

[24] *Ibid.*, p. 117.
[25] William Butler Yeats, *The Tower* (New York: Macmillan, 1929), p. 14.
[26] *The Romantic Survival*, p. 63.
[27] *Ibid.*, p. 64.
[28] "Shelley, Dryden, and Mr. Eliot, "*Rehabilitations*, pp. 26-27.
[29] Auden's essay in *The Intent of the Critic*, edited by Donald A. Stauffer
(Princeton: Princeton, 1941), p. 137.

Contemporary modifications and aberrations of Romanticism

Romanticism has hardly been fallow in the fiction of our time, even in those writers we normally take to be Realists. Nathan Starr points out that while dealing in "realistic" material, writers like Hemingway, Steinbeck, and Faulkner reflect "assumptions about experience which link . . . [them] with the Romantics of the nineteenth century."[30] The result is an emphasis on intuition and instinctual response, frequently "a new kind of 'gothic' terror," recognition of the strange yet close relation between man and nature, and something of the old Romantic intensity with regard to one's art. Because fiction has largely replaced poetry as the dominant genre, it has taken over certain poetic methods which facilitate this approach—e.g., the stream-of-consciousness technique in Woolf, Joyce, and Faulkner, which provides "the kind of spontaneous, intuitive release of feeling which we usually associate with poetry."[31]

There are also numerous writers who are obviously Romantic in at least one important aspect of their work. What could be more Romantic than the novels of Thomas Wolfe or those passages in Joyce or Katherine Mansfield which reflect the kind of radiant exultation one associates with Emily Brontë or Meredith? One finds both Romantic longing and exultation in the novels of Joyce Cary, T. H. White, Charles Williams and J. R. R. Tolkien. Sherwood Anderson and F. Scott Fitzgerald treat love between the sexes in highly mystical fashion. Sinclair Lewis tells of a Fairy Child who keeps alive longing even in a Babbitt. And Joseph Conrad set out deliberately to recover in fiction the old Romantic awe, wonder, and sense of expansion. The same might be said of novelists like James Branch Cabell, who revolted against what they regarded as the "no-exit"

---

[30] Nathan Comfort Starr, "The Romantic Realists," *EIEAKU*, Kansai University, Osaka, Japan, 1 (June, 1954), 179f.

[31] *Ibid.*, p. 183.

kind of realism which flourished in the earlier part of the century.[32]

Among the poets, Dylan Thomas appears the most violent and haunting of the new Romantics, Yeats perhaps the most deeply satisfying, and Auden the most provocative. But there are others whose work is conspicuously Romantic in spirit and treatment: Edna St. Vincent Millay, Christopher Fry, Walter de la Mare, Robert Bridges, John Masefield, Wallace Stevens, and Theodore Roethke.

Thus, I would say that Romanticism has survived first through the reaction against theories which temporarily threatened it (the "realist" movement in fiction, the "poem as machine" approach). This reaction called for a recovery of the old Romantic awe before one's material and a desire for the Romantic sense of expansion.

The second mode of survival is quite different. It stems from the Art for Art's Sake movement of the nineteenth century and particularly from Walter Pater. As Bayley points out, Pater virtually reversed the idea that the imagination has a unifying power over external phenomena. He urged a new sensibility which would allow the artist to ignore the objective world (which, in his view, is falsely objectified by language) and concentrate on the "unstable, flickering, inconsistent" impressions "which burn and are extinguished with our consciousness of them."[33] This almost solipsistic view of the imagination influenced both Yeats, in his conception of the poet's Masks, and Virginia Woolf, who carried the "Paterian consciousness" (Bayley's term) one stage further, attempting to dispense with the problems of individuality in such a way that "there is no character in the accepted sense and therefore no 'I' and 'Not-I.' "[34] Bayley also discusses Proust in this connection. This approach often includes a curious distrust of love and religion (which the older Romantics associated

[32] See David Daiches' essays on Conrad and Mansfield in *The Novel and the Modern World* (Chicago: U. of Chicago, 1939).

[33] Quoted from Pater's epilogue to *The Renaissance* in Bayley, p. 46.

[34] *The Romantic Survival*, p. 47.

with the imagination) and even pleasure—Lewis has observed that "Pater prepared for pleasure as if it were martyrdom."[35] Yet these writers believed ardently in what Bayley calls "the mysteriously intercommunicable power of aesthetic experience." They cannot quite give up the Romantic view of the imagination; yet they cannot keep it as it was in Wordsworth and Coleridge. And so by daring experiment or brilliantly winnowing analysis they seek to retain the Romantic sense of mystery and aspiration.

The third mode of survival, as I see it, has been explored in a book by Mario Praz, *The Romantic Agony*. It consists of making a pseudo-religion out of Romanticism, worshipping the dark gods of the soul. Praz has pertinent discussions of Baudelaire, Swinburne, Yeats, and D. H. Lawrence in this regard. Some have viewed the private religions of Yeats and Lawrence with horror. I do not share this view. Granting that there may well be something aberrant in these writers, I believe nevertheless that they are seeking to reestablish the association of certain feelings (awe, longing, mystery) with physical sensation and with the beauty, wonder, and terror of human existence. In so doing they react against any concept of religion which would reduce it to dogma or morality. They have glimpsed the dark side of God and felt the mysterious pulse of life. They want concreteness, genuine feeling, amplitude where so many modern developments have forced upon us abstraction, "mental" feelings, and narrowness. They want spontaneity in place of the paralyzing self-consciousness and unending analysis of top-heavy intellectualism.

This seems to be what many of the "Beat" artists and intellectuals of the fifties were looking for also—that elusive but highly satisfying sense of meaningful mystery. Jack Kerouac and Clellon Holmes described their lives as a search for the Beatific Vision.[36] One sees this search in the

[35] "Christianity and Literature," in *Rehabilitations*, p. 196; also in *Christian Reflections*, p. 10.

[36] See *The Beat Generation and the Angry Young Men*, edited by Gene Feldman and Max Gartenberg (New York: Citadel, 1958).

LSD "trippers" of the sixties. It is there in many of the most popular films such as *Dr. Zhivago* and *Love Story,* in the Hari Krishna mystics, the Transcendental Meditation Society, and the body cultists who are looking for a depth dimension in sex and health. One sees it also in the scores of popular songs which seek to elevate a love affair to the *summum bonum:*

> Some want something they can't explain—
> As they climb the Ladder of Love.

Hence the desperate ambivalence of our age.[37] The fruits of scientific inquiry, of technology, of concentrating upon the "empirical" realities leave a dryness in the soul. If one is a thorough enough Materialist, Romantic feelings (except perhaps where sex is concerned) "become equated with nonsense and unreality, and yet such unreality is all that poetry has to work on."[38]

The value of Lewis' concept

I see all these modes of Romantic survival as evidence for Lewis' theory of *Sehnsucht.* For it is *Sehnsucht* which binds together such diverse writers as Dylan Thomas (his "Fern Hill" is a beautiful statement of it), Edna St. Vincent Millay ("O World I Cannot Hold Thee Close Enough"), and D. H. Lawrence ("the humming of unseen harps within us"). It is *Sehnsucht* which both expresses and helps to satisfy longing and the desire for mystery. It

[37] The Vedantist movement among British and American intellectuals seems also to reflect this desperate ambivalence. It might be thought of as a more sophisticated form of the "Beat" and later the "Hippie" trends among the younger generation. It is significant that writers like Aldous Huxley and Christopher Isherwood should turn to the religions of the East (especially Hinduism) in their desire to retain the soul. In fact, one might interpret Vedantism as an attempt to face *Sehnsucht* honestly. What the Vedantist seeks to do, of course, is to renounce longing. But he may actually concentrate on it, by a kind of ultimate inversion of his renunciation of desire, and thus to be nourished by it—in the same way a Christian is nourished by a sense of sin. The individual faces the threat and relies on something beyond himself to overcome it. Thus he is able to deal more fully with the data of experience and yet transcend them.

[38] Bayley, *The Romantic Survival,* p. 79.

has been present in every age, but it seems to be far more obvious in our time than in any previous period. It defies any final definition or analysis, and yet if we avoid considering it on these grounds, we fail to deal with an exciting and crucial concept.

Lewis' explanation of *Sehnsucht* reveals to me a basic continuity between nineteenth- and twentieth-century literature. For if we use *Sehnsucht* as a touchstone of the Romantic attitude, we discover that the various writers discussed in this chapter share one thing in common: an interest in that dimension of experience which gives rise to nostalgia and longing, the dimension which fascinated Coleridge and Wordsworth. Where this interest is intense— as in Thomas Wolfe or Dylan Thomas—we can call the writer Romantic without fear of contradiction. Where this interest is expressed with less intensity or is partly obscured by other emphases—as in T. S. Eliot or Virginia Woolf—we can speak of Romantic elements only with careful qualification. But the continuity remains—evidence of the basic strength of the Romantic attitude, evidence also of the amazingly similar focus taken by so much of human experience. I might add: evidence as well, by reason of its prevalence in our time, that the bewilderingly new developments witnessed by our century seem to encourage this preoccupation with longing. But I will rest my case just short of this point, for it is not essential to the main thesis of this chapter—i.e., that Lewis' concept of *Sehnsucht* provides a key to understanding the New Romanticism, that it suggests a useful and illuminating approach to modern literature.

All this is not, however, to make any brief for the Romantic temper in and for itself. As David Daiches has said so well: "Romanticism is an effect and not a cause, a result of value and not a source of value."[39] Many writers became disillusioned with Romanticism in the twentieth century precisely because they expected too much of it. Lewis retained his faith in the basic validity of Romantic literature because he believed it was compatible with a

[39] *The Novel and the Modern World*, p. 202.

Christian ontology. The sense of nostalgia cannot be valued for itself, at least not for long. *Sehnsucht* has genuine meaning only in an ontology which has a place for it.

VIII EPILOGUE

Lewis as a Christian theorist

Lewis seeks to persuade neither by sentiment nor by cold reason but by a combination of reason and feeling. Unlike Charles Williams in whom feeling was stronger than thinking, Lewis keeps a balance between the two. As Hillegas points out in *Shadows of Imagination* (p. 11), it was the combination of Kirk's logic and Macdonald's transcendent intuitions which shaped Lewis' mature sensibility. Lewis rejects the cognitive-emotive disjunction argument, holding that though poetic language does express emotion, this does not mean it has no claim to truth. He accepts the scientific-poetic dichotomy but *not* the cognitive-emotive one. By his respect for reason and for the world of Fact, he is able to give his novels clean edges and clarity not to be found in the more ambiguous work of Macdonald and Williams.

In Lewis we sometimes think we are listening to an argument, but as Austin Farrer reminds us, we are in fact being presented with a vision, and it is the vision which carries conviction.[1] Gunnar Urang agrees, maintaining that as strongly as Lewis applies logic in his expository passages, it is the imaginative appeals that stick with us.

If it is the calling of each author to make some one

[1] "The Christian Apologist" in *Light on C. S. Lewis*, edited by Jocelyn Gibb (New York: Harcourt, Brace), p. 37.

point well and memorably, then the point we shall recall for C. S. Lewis is his case for the feeling intellect. As Chapters II and III point out, he was peculiarly prepared for this mission. His literary favorites all contain the golden skein of longing—*The Fairy Queen, Paradise Lost,* Blake, Sir Walter Scott, Meredith, Morris, and Williams. And he early discovered that what truly moves the conscience is not so much a sense of wrongdoing as a feeling of loss. As James Higgins says in his discussion of Macdonald, "Sorrow springs not so much from pity or guilt as from love. To teach someone to be sorrowful, to ask someone to repent, one must first teach him to know and love goodness."[2]

To awaken a desire for love and goodness this was Lewis' purpose in almost everything he wrote. And, according to Higgins, the love one finds in Lewis' books is not the "spongy emotion which self-indulgent man sometimes invents for his own pleasure. It is the hard, painful, overwhelming love for which man has been grasping since the beginning of time." Then Higgins adds: "What a coming down it is for the little girl who has met love in its varied and splendid forms . . . [in the world of faerie] and who settles for that which she finds between the covers of *True Romance* in later years."[3]

What Lewis sets out to do he does well. His only serious weakness is, Pelagian-like, trying too hard. As Gunnar Urang observes, Lewis finds it difficult "to confine himself to merely baptizing his reader's imagination. Perhaps he wishes to confirm him as well" (p. 38). Occasionally his imaginative works are overloaded with meanings and subliminal echoes of meaning. His earnestness sometimes leads him to caricature in his fictional characters (character being the most difficult aspect of fiction for Lewis). And in *Mere Christianity,* his radio talks, he does not pause for qualifications and nuances of idea as carefully as in his other books. Lewis recognized the danger of overzealousness and self-assurance and wrote poignantly of it in "The Apologist's Evening Prayer":

2 *Beyond Words*, p. 68.
3 *Ibid.,* p. 39.

From all my lame defeats and oh! much more
From all the victories that I seemed to score;
From cleverness shot forth on Thy behalf
At which, while angels weep, the audience laugh;
From all my proofs of Thy divinity,
Thou, who wouldst give no sign, deliver me.
Thoughts are but coins. Let me not trust, instead
Of Thee, their thin-worn image of Thy head.
From all my thoughts, even from my thoughts of Thee,
O thou fair Silence, fall, and set me free.
Lord of the narrow gate and the needle's eye.
Take from me all my trumpery lest I die.

The function of Sehnsucht

What then shall we finally make of this transcendent joy
which comes to us always as a cosmic pointer, telling us it
is not joy we want but urging always beyond. Lewis, as I
read him, never clearly resolves how important Joy-
Longing is theologically. He insists that longing, conscience, and myth contain divine revelation, yet they do
not have the same *objective* value as the revelation in
Christ, though especially for those who have not heard of
Christ, they have *subjective* value.

As Urang points out, the crucial question is: Does this
romantic experience mediate revelatory reality or merely
reflect it? In cold prose Lewis seems to take a negative
view, claiming for *Sehnsucht* only a reflective function.
But his fictional and poetic images give it a greater import
than that, suggesting that there is indeed revelatory reality
in *Sehnsucht*.

This archetype which is so potently endowed with "the
tug of the transcendent," to use R. W. B. Lewis' phrase,
gets spent and misspent on indulgent emotionalism. It gets
debased by trite and sentimental use, as in pulp fiction and
popular music. But the romantic muse is still called to be a
handmaiden of the Lord, and in the service of great mystics like Francis, St. Teresa, and Evelyn Underhill, the
Maid of Longing dances wildly but chastely in praise to
God. She nourishes us more than we realize, for our
taproots which go deep in the soil draw upon the secret

mysteries which she provides. As uncomfortable as *Sehnsucht* sometimes makes us, would we willingly dispense with this special awareness?

Lewis is above all a master of the Way of Affirmations. He says in *Arthurian Torso*: "Every created thing is, in its degree, an image of God, and the ordinate and faithful appreciation of that thing is a clue which, truly followed, will lead back to Him" (p. 151). But it may be a circuitous journey.

We live now "amid all the anomalies, inconveniences, hopes, and excitements of a house that is being rebuilt" (*Miracles,* p. 159). The Day is coming, however, when we will join in a great cosmic dance or ride magnificent stallions through the heavens, when we will have reached the individuation we have longed for, and when the cord of longing will lead directly to Him who bids us be one with Him in a great mutuality of loves. As Lewis puts it in a paragraph which he pencilled on a fly-leaf of his copy of von Hügel's *Eternal Life:*

> It is not an abstraction called Humanity that is to be saved. It is you, . . . your soul, and, in some sense yet to be understood, even your body, that was made for the high and holy place. All that you are . . . every fold and crease of your individuality was devised from all eternity to fit God as a glove fits a hand. All that intimate particularity which you can hardly grasp yourself, much less communicate to your fellow creatures, is no mystery to Him. He made those ins and outs that He might fill them. Then He gave your soul so curious a life because it is the key designed to unlock that door, of all the myriad doors in Him.

That we have appetites suggests we will find food. That we get drowsy suggests that sleep exists. That we respond to melody suggests that men will devise music. That we are haunted by unquenchable longings points to a goal for that longing—in eternity if not in time. I find in C. S. Lewis' understanding of *Sehnsucht* a parallel to Anselm's ontological argument, Lewis' most significant contribution to Christian apologetics, and an important clue for understanding literary history.

The Well at the World's End, the Green Hills Beyond,

Shangri-La, El Dorado, Narnia—Lewis believes these are all splashes of Godlight in the dark wood of our life. Is there any better explanation or one which can be applied to more cases?

In my mind none of the rival theories does justice to the data nor does any of them take aesthetic experience as seriously as does Lewis' interpretation. Hence, we have yet another instance of something whose ultimacy is challenged by religious faith, being given, on a new basis, a high regard. Lewis can take aesthetic experience seriously because he does not make it into a religion. By interpreting the aesthetic "under the aspect of eternity," he is able to let the experience be itself.

It points to a Great Dance, yes, and to the Lord of the Dance, but it also provides the first halting steps of that exultant movement and our feet can begin now to learn its figures and its rhythm.

Selected Bibliography

I. Books by C. S. Lewis

I have included both British and American editions. In some cases the pagination differs. Many of Lewis' books are available in paperback editions. For a more complete listing of Lewis' works, see Walter Hooper's bibliography in *Light on C. S. Lewis*, edited by Jocelyn Gibb.

The Abolition of Man, or, Reflections on Education with Special Reference to the Teaching of English in the Upper Forms of Schools, Riddell Memorial Lectures, Fifteenth Series. London: Oxford University Press, 1943; Geoffrey Bles, 1946; New York: Macmillan, 1947.

The Allegory of Love: A Study in Medieval Tradition. London: Oxford University Press, 1936 (reprinted with corrections in 1938).

Arthurian Torso: Containing the Posthumous Fragment The Figure of Arthur *by Charles Williams and a Commentary on the Arthurian Poems of Charles Williams by C. S. Lewis*. London: Oxford University Press, 1948; Wm. B. Eerdmans, 1974. The Eerdmans edition is part of a volume also including *Taliessin Through Logres* and *The Region of the Summer Stars*, two collections of Arthurian poems by Charles Williams.

Beyond Personality. London: Geoffrey Bles, 1944; New York: Macmillan, 1945. Included in *Mere Christianity*.

The Case for Christianity. New York: Macmillan, 1943. Published in

166

Britain as *Broadcast Talks: Reprinted with Some Alterations from Two Series of Broadcast Talks . . . Given in 1941 and 1942*. London: Geoffrey Bles, 1942. Included in *Mere Christianity*.

Christian Behaviour: A Further Series of Broadcast Talks. London: Geoffrey Bles, 1943; New York: Macmillan, 1943. Included in *Mere Christianity*.

Dymer, under the pseudonym of Clive Hamilton. London: J. M. Dent and Sons, 1926; New York: E. P. Dutton, 1926. Reprinted with a new preface in *Narrative Poems*. New York: Macmillan, 1950.

English Literature in the Sixteenth Century, Excluding Drama. Oxford: Clarendon Press, 1954.

An Experiment in Criticism. Cambridge: Cambridge University Press, 1961.

The Four Loves. London: Geoffrey Bles, 1960; New York: Harcourt, Brace, 1960.

George Macdonald: An Anthology. London: Geoffrey Bles, 1946; New York: Macmillan, 1947.

God in the Dock. Grand Rapids: Wm. B. Eerdmans, 1970. Published in England as *Undeceptions*. London: Geoffrey Bles, 1970.

The Great Divorce: A Dream. London: Geoffrey Bles, 1945; New York: Macmillan, 1946.

The Horse and His Boy. London: Geoffrey Bles, 1954; New York: Macmillan, 1954.

The Last Battle: A Story for Children. London: Geoffrey Bles, 1955; Bodley Head, 1956; New York: Macmillan, 1956; Harcourt, Brace, 1956.

Letters to Malcolm: Chiefly on Prayer. London: Geoffrey Bles, 1964; New York: Harcourt, Brace, 1964.

The Lion, the Witch, and the Wardrobe. London: Geoffrey Bles, 1950: New York: Macmillan, 1950.

The Magician's Nephew. London: Bodley Head, 1955; New York: Macmillan, 1955.

Mere Christianity: a revised and amplified edition, with a new introduction, of the three books *Broadcast Talks, Christian Behaviour,* and *Beyond Personality*. London: Geoffrey Bles, 1952; New York: Macmillan, 1953.

Miracles: A Preliminary Study. London: Geoffrey Bles, 1947; New York: Macmillan, 1947. Reprinted with a revision of chapter 3 by Fontana, 1960.

Of Other Worlds, edited by Walter Hooper. New York: Harcourt, Brace, 1966.

Out of the Silent Planet. London: John Lane, 1938; New York: Macmillan, 1943.

Perelandra. London: John Lane, 1943; New York: Macmillan, 1944.

(With E. M. W. Tillyard), *The Personal Heresy: A Controversy.* London: Oxford University Press, 1939.

The Pilgrim's Regress: An Allegorical Apology for Christianity, Reason and Romanticism. London: J. M. Dent and Sons, 1933; London: Sheed and Ward, 1935; London: Geoffrey Bles, 1943; Grand Rapids: Wm. B. Eerdmans, 1958. The latter two editions contain an author's preface, footnotes, and running headlines.

Poems, edited by Walter Hooper. London: Geoffrey Bles, 1964; New York: Harcourt, Brace, 1965.

A Preface to Paradise Lost: Being the Ballard Matthews Lectures Delivered at University College, North Wales, 1941, Revised and Enlarged. London: Oxford University Press, 1942.

Prince Caspian. London: Geoffrey Bles, 1951; New York: Macmillan, 1951.

The Problem of Pain. London: Geoffrey Bles, 1940; New York: Macmillan, 1943.

Reflections on the Psalms. London: Geoffrey Bles, 1958; New York: Harcourt, Brace, 1958.

Rehabilitations and Other Essays. London: Oxford University Press, 1939. Six of these nine essays appear in *Selected Literary Essays by C. S. Lewis,* edited by Walter Hooper. Cambridge: Cambridge University Press, 1969.

Spirits in Bondage, under the pseudonym of Clive Hamilton. London: William Heinemann, 1919.

Screwtape Letters. London: Geoffrey Bles, 1942; New York: Macmillan, 1943. Also published with a new preface and "Screwtape Proposes a Toast," Macmillan.

The Silver Chair. London: Geoffrey Bles, 1953; New York: Macmillan, 1953.

Surprised by Joy: The Shape of My Early Life. London: Geoffrey Bles, 1955; New York: Harcourt, Brace, 1956.

That Hideous Strength: A Modern Fairy-Tale for Grown-ups. London: John Lane, 1945; New York: Macmillan, 1946.

Till We Have Faces: A Myth Retold. London: Geoffrey Bles, 1956; Grand Rapids: Wm. B. Eerdmans, 1966.

The Voyage of the "Dawn Treader." London: Geoffrey Bles, 1952; New York: Macmillan, 1952.

The Weight of Glory and Other Addresses. Grand Rapids: Eerdmans, 1965. Published in Britain as *Transposition and Other Addresses.* London: Geoffrey Bles, 1949.

II. Essays and Prefaces by C. S. Lewis

De Descriptione Temporum, an Inaugural Lecture. Cambridge: Cambridge University Press, 1955. Also in *Selected Literary Essays.*

"A Dream," *Spectator,* 173 (July 28, 1944), 77.

Hero and Leander: Wharton Lecture on English Poetry, British Academy. London: Oxford University Press, 1952. Also in *Selected Literary Essays.*

"Lilies That Fester," *Twentieth Century,* 157 (April, 1955), 330-341.

"The Personal Heresy in Criticism," and "Open Letter to Dr. Tillyard," *Essays and Reviews by Members of the English Association,* 19 (1934) and 21 (1936). These two essays later appeared in the book, *The Personal Heresy,* written with E. M. W. Tillyard.

Preface to *Essays Presented to Charles Williams,* written by Dorothy Sayers and others. London: Oxford University Press, 1947; Grand Rapids: Wm. B. Eerdmans, 1966. Also contains an essay by Lewis, "On Stories."

Preface to *The Hierarchy of Heaven and Earth: A New Diagram of Man in the Universe* by D. E. Harding. London: Faber & Faber, 1952; New York: Harper, 1952.

Preface to *The Incarnation of the Word of God: Being the Treatise of St. Athanasius De Incarnatione Verbi Dei,* translated by a Religious of C.S.M.V.S.Th. London: Geoffrey Bles, 1944; New York: Macmillan, 1946.

"Psycho-analysis and Literary Criticism," *Essays and Studies by Members of the English Association,* 27 (1942), 7-21. Also in *Selected Literary Essays.*

"A Rejoinder to Dr. Pittenger," *Christian Century,* 48 (Nov. 26, 1958), 1359-1361. Also in *God in the Dock.* Grand Rapids: Wm. B. Eerdmans, 1970.

"Sometimes Fairy Stories May Say Best What's Best To Be Said," *New York Times Book Review, Children's Book Section,* Nov. 18, 1956, p. 3.

"Will We Lose God in Outer Space?" *Christian Herald* (April, 1958), pp. 19f.

III. Critical Material on C. S. Lewis

Allen, E. L. "The Theology of C. S. Lewis," *Modern Churchman,* 34 (Jan.-March, 1945), 318.

Anderson, G. C. "C. S. Lewis: Foe of Humanism," *Christian Century,* 63 (Dec. 25, 1946), 1562-1563.

Atkins, Gaius G. "The Great Invasion," *Christian Century,* 64 (Dec. 3, 1947), 1486-1487.

Auden, W. H. Review of The Great Divorce, *Saturday Review of Literature,* 29 (April 13, 1946), 42.

Bacon, Leonard. Review of Screwtape Letters, *Saturday Review of Literature,* 26 (April 17, 1943), 20.

Beaton, Cecil W. H., and Kenneth Tynan, *Persona Grata.* London: Putnam, 1954.

Boss, Edgar W. *The Theology of C. S. Lewis.* Unpublished doctoral thesis done at Northern Baptist Theological Seminary in Chicago, 1948.

Brady, Charles A. "Finding God in Narnia," *America,* 96 (Oct. 27, 1956), 103-105. See also D. Keith Mano's review of the Narnian chronicles, *New York Times,* Feb. 21, 1971.

———. "Introduction to Lewis," *America,* May 27, 1944, and June 10, 1944.

Cooke, Alistair. "Mr. Anthony at Oxford," *New Republic,* 110 (April 24, 1944), 580.

Cunningham, Larry. *C. S. Lewis: Defender of the Faith.* Philadelphia: Westminster Press, 1967.

Curley, Thomas F. "Myth Into Novel," *Commonweal,* 65 (Feb. 8, 1957), 494-495.

Davis, Robert Gorham. "Cupid and Psyche," *New York Times Book Review,* Jan. 13, 1957, p. 5.

Davidman, Joy. "The Longest Way Round," in *These Found the Way,* edited by David W. Soper. Philadelphia: Westminster Press, 1951.

"Don vs. Devil," *Time,* 50 (Sept. 8, 1947), 65-66f.

Driberg, Tom. "Lobbies of the Soul," *New Statesman,* 49 (March 19, 1955), 393-394.

Empson, William. Review of The Allegory of Love, *Spectator,* 157 (Sept. 4, 1936), 389.

Fowler, Helen. "C. S. Lewis: Sputnik or Dinosaur," *Approach: A Literary Quarterly,* Summer, 1959, pp. 8-14.

Fremantle, Anne. Review of Beyond Personality, *Commonweal,* 42 (Sept. 14, 1945), 528f.

———. Review of Surprised By Joy, *Commonweal,* 63 (Feb. 3, 1956), 464-465.

———. Review of That Hideous Strength, *New York Herald Tribune Weekly Book Review,* June 2, 1946, p. 12.

Fuller, Edmund. "The Christian Spaceman—C. S. Lewis," *Horizon: A Magazine of the Arts,* 1 (May, 1959), 64-69f.

———. Review of The Magician's Nephew, *Chicago Sunday Tribune Magazine of Books,* Nov. 13, 1955, p. 36.

———. Review of Till We Have Faces, *Chicago Sunday Tribune Magazine of Books,* Jan. 20, 1957, p. 2.

Gardner, F. M. "L. A. Carnegie Medal Award for 1956," *Library Association Record,* 59 (May, 1957), 168-169.

Gibb, Jocelyn, ed. *Light on C. S. Lewis.* New York: Harcourt, Brace, 1965.

Gilbert, A. H. "Critics of Mr. C. S. Lewis on Milton's Satan," *South Atlantic Quarterly,* 47 (April, 1948), 216-225.

Gilbert, Douglas, and Kilby, Clyde S. *C. S. Lewis: Images of His World.* Grand Rapids, Wm. B. Eerdmans, 1973.

Gill, Theodore A. "Not Quite All," *Christian Century,* 73 (May 9, 1956), 585.

Green, Roger Lancelyn. *Tellers of Tales.* London: British Book Centre, 1954.

Grennan, M. B. "Lewis' Trilogy: A Scholar's Holiday," *Catholic World,* 167 (July, 1948), 337-344.

Griffiths, Dom Bede. *The Golden String.* New York: P. J. Kenedy and Sons, 1955.

Hailsham, Lord. "Dr. Lewis' Pilgrimage," *Spectator,* 195 (Dec. 9, 1955), 805-806.

Haldane, J. B. S. "God and Mr. C. S. Lewis," *The Rationalist Annual for the Year 1948,* edited by Frederick Watts. London: Watts.

Hamm, Victor M. "Mr. Lewis in Perelandra," *Thought: Fordham University Quarterly,* 20 (June, 1945), 271-290.

Harrison, Charles A. "The Renaissance Epitomized," *Sewanee Review,* 63 (Winter, 1955), 53-61.

Hartshorne, Charles. "Philosophy and Orthodoxy," *Ethics,* 54 (July, 1944), 295-298.

Higgins, James. *Beyond Words: Mystical Fancy in Children's Literature.* New York: Teachers College Press, 1970.

Hillegas, Mark. *Shadows of Imagination: the Fantasy of C. S. Lewis, J. R. R. Tolkien, and Charles Williams.* Carbondale: Southern Illinois University Press, 1969.

Hough, Graham. "Old Western Man," *Twentieth Century,* 157 (Feb., 1955), 102-110.

Huttar, Charles A., ed. *Imagination and the Spirit: Essays in Literature and the Christian Faith Presented to Clyde S. Kilby.* Grand Rapids: Wm. B. Eerdmans, 1971.

Kilby, Clyde S. *The Christian World of C. S. Lewis.* Grand Rapids: Wm. B. Eerdmans, 1964.

———. "C. S. Lewis and His Critics," *Christianity Today,* 3 (Dec. 8, 1958), 13-15.

———. Review of Surprised by Joy, *New York Herald Tribune Book Review,* Feb. 5, 1956, p. 5.

Kreeft, Peter. *C. S. Lewis* (in *Contemporary Writers in Christian Perspective* series), edited by Roderick Jellema. Grand Rapids: Wm. B. Eerdmans, 1969.

Lindskoog, Kathryn. *The Lion of Judah in Never-Never Land.* Grand Rapids: Wm. B. Eerdmans, 1973.

Masterman, Margaret. "C. S. Lewis: the Author and the Hero," *Twentieth Century,* 158 (Dec., 1955), 539-548.

Meyers, Edward O. "The Religious Works of C. S. Lewis," *Theology Today,* 1 (1944), 545f.

Moorman, Charles. *The Precincts of Felicity: The Augustinian City of the Oxford Christians.* Gainesville: University of Florida Press, 1966.

Morley, Christopher. Review of Out of the Silent Planet, *Commonweal,* 39 (Oct. 29, 1943), 45.

Myres, John L. Review of Miracles, *Nature,* 160 (Aug. 30, 1947), 275-276.

New Yorker, Review of The Lion, the Witch, and the Wardrobe, 26 (Dec. 2, 1950), 177.

Paulding, Gouverneur. "The Most Dejected and Reluctant Convert," *Reporter,* 14 (March 8, 1956), 45-46.

Pittenger, W. Norman. "A Critique of C. S. Lewis," *Christian Century,* 75 (Oct. 1, 1958), 1104-1107.

Reilly, R. J. *Romantic Religion: A Study of Owen Barfield, C. S. Lewis, Charles Williams, and J. R. R. Tolkien.* Athens: University of Georgia Press, 1971.

Rolo, C. J. Review of Till We Have Faces, *Atlantic Monthly,* 199 (Feb., 1957), 84.

Saurat, Denis. Review of A Preface to Paradise Lost, *New Statesman and Nation,* 24 (Nov. 14, 1942), 325.

Schuster, G. N. Review of The Problem of Pain, *New York Herald Tribune Weekly Book Review,* Dec. 26, 1943, p. 6.

Shumaker, Wayne. "Cosmic Trilogy of C. S. Lewis," *Hudson Review,* 8 (Summer, 1955), 240-254.

Soper, David Wesley. "An Interview With C. S. Lewis," *Zion's Herald,* Jan. 14, 1948, pp. 28-29f and continued in the Jan. 21 issue, pp. 61f.

Spencer, Theodore. "Symbols of a Good and Bad England," *New York Times Book Review,* July 7, 1946, p. 10.

Starr, Nathan C. *King Arthur Today: The Arthurian Legend in English and American Literature, 1901-1953.* Gainesville: University of Florida Press, 1954.

———. *C. S. Lewis's "Till We Have Faces."* New York: Seabury Press, 1968.

Stoll, E. E. "Give the Devil His Due: A Reply to Mr. Lewis," *Review of English Studies,* 20 (April, 1944), 108-124.

Sugrue, Thomas. Review of The Great Divorce, *New York Herald Tribune Weekly Book Review,* March 3, 1946, p. 4.

Tolkien, J. R. R. *Beowulf: the Monsters and the Critics.* London: British Academy Proceedings, 1936.

Trowbridge, Clinton. *The Twentieth Century British Supernatural Novel.* Doctoral thesis done at the University of Florida, 1958. Library of Congress Card No. Mic. 58-1540.

Urang, Gunnar. *Shadows of Heaven: Religion and Fantasy in the Writing of C. S. Lewis, Charles Williams, and J. R. R. Tolkien.* Phildelphia: Pilgrim Press, 1971.

Wagenknecht, Edward. Review of A Preface to Paradise Lost, *New York Times,* May 23, 1943, p. 10.

Wain, John. Review of English Literature in the Sixteenth Century, *Spectator,* 193 (Oct. 1, 1954), 403-405.

Walsh, Chad. *C. S. Lewis: Apostle to the Skeptics.* New York: Macmillan, 1949.

———. "Pro's and Con's of C. S. Lewis," *Religion in Life,* 18 (Spring, 1949), 222-228.

———. Review of The Lion, the Witch, and the Wardrobe, *New York Times,* Nov. 12, 1950, p. 20.

———. Review of Miracles, *New York Times,* Sept. 28, 1947, p. 5.

———. Review of Surprised By Joy, *Saturday Review of Literature,* 39 (March 3, 1956), 32-33.

———. Review of Till We Have Faces, *New York Herald Tribune Weekly Book Review,* Jan. 20, 1957, p. 3.

White, William Luther. *The Image of Man in C. S. Lewis.* Nashville: Abingdon Press, 1969.

Index

See also contents and entries in the bibliography.